A Fulhamish Coming of Age

A Fulhamish Coming of Age

FULHAM IN EUROPE
1973–2003

Alex Ferguson
—The Traveller

ASHWATER PRESS

Also by Alex Ferguson:

Pandora's Fulhamish Box
(published March 2003)

First published in February 2005

Designed and published by
Ashwater Press
68 Tranmere Road, Whitton, Twickenham, Middlesex, TW2 7JB

Printed and bound by Butler and Tanner, Frome, Somerset

ISBN 0 953884 9 0

CONTENTS

INTRODUCTION

The account that follows is unofficial, though factually definitive. It chronicles thirty years spent watching Fulham Football Club competing in recognised UEFA competitions in Europe. There are twenty-three games in all, comprising Anglo-Italian Tournament, Intertoto, UEFA Cup and UEFA Women's Cup fixtures.

The matches plus various anecdotes surrounding them have been recorded in the usual Fulhamish manner. This approach has ensured that the statistical details have been captured for posterity.

With the club's future currently looking bright let us hope that there are many more European games to come. And soon. A second volume perhaps? Who knows? Such is the glorious uncertainty surrounding association football.

Alex Ferguson, Feltham, January 2005.

Happiness is: Watching one's only son making his way in the world
...and Fulham Football Club returning to Craven Cottage.

1: AU REVOIR

My faithful ancestral friend. Rest assured, we shall return. Meanwhile, let us revel in what is today. Rejoice in how far this beloved club of ours has come in just over half a decade. Six short years to journey from the depths. When it is done and we walk away, our heads will be held high. No regrets at closing the door on our heritage. Instead a marvellous panorama of memories…

Of Fulham's opponents for the second foray into the Intertoto competition, little was known beforehand. A miniscule amount was forthcoming. A further problem presented itself. How to correctly spell their name when transposed into Roman script. Aigaleo, Aegaleo or even Egaleo were all in the frame. Linguistic skills were called for. A straight transliteration from the ancient symbology shows it to be the first on the list. Aigaleo it is then.

Only Fulhamish can do that to you. Research on their city of origin revealed that they were one of the lesser known outfits operating out of Athens. Almost as many league clubs there as in London. AEK, Akratitos, Apollon, Athinaikos, Ethnikos, Olympiakos, Panathinaikos, Panionios, Proodeftiki. And Aigaleo. Whatever. A rough, tough pedigree to be overcome for sure.

Yet there was still sufficient interest in the novelty of the fixture for over five thousand souls to attend. The Stevenage Road, enclosure and Riverside stands were well populated for another sun-drenched European affair. Could Fulham set the seal on the supposed final game at Craven Cottage with a well earned victory?

Being as it was their first venture into European competition, the blues of Aigaleo City were not about to make things easy for our favourites. Adopting a cautious approach from the outset, they strung a stifling blockade of bodies across the midfield and invited Fulham to break it down. It wasn't particularly pretty stuff to watch. Indeed, it became a rather frustrating afternoon. The type of event that one would prefer to forget but, because of the occasion, could not. The Greeks' physical approach sadly appeared to be just part of their national game. Even more infuriating was the fact that their aggressive and combative style of play was tolerated by a more than lenient set of Belgian match officials. The final outcome of a running battle of attrition was the brandishing of only three yellow cards. A regrettable indictment to set before the hallowed portals of Craven Cottage.

Yet out of adversity came a shaft of light. Enough to send the travelling faithful forward towards Athens with an eternal springing in both their step and savage breast. Please excuse the mixed metaphors. Attempts on goal were at a

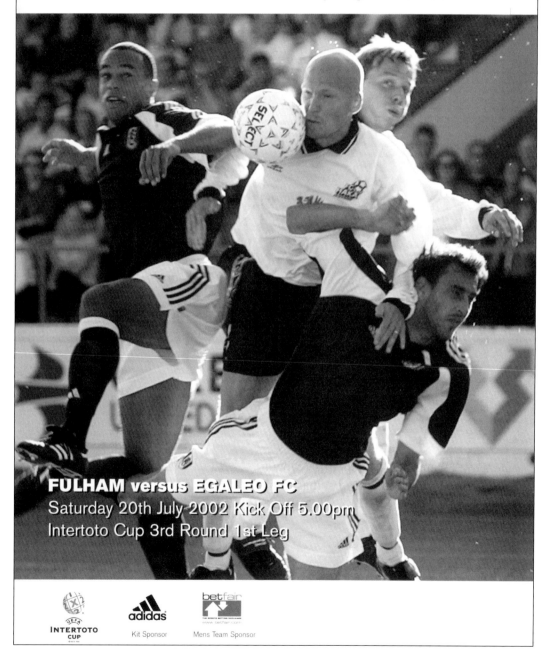

FULHAM

Your Official Fulham FC Matchday Programme £1.00

FULHAM versus EGALEO FC
Saturday 20th July 2002 Kick Off 5.00pm
Intertoto Cup 3rd Round 1st Leg

INTERTOTO CUP

adidas
Kit Sponsor

betfair
Mens Team Sponsor

premium over the ninety minutes but there were two efforts that require description. During the first half Steed Malbranque managed to tickle the woodwork with a half chance. Then, twelve minutes from the end of the game, just when the majority of the crowd were beginning to doubt whether Fulham would ever breach the Greek barricades, came the moment. A vindication of our patience. An inch perfect through ball from Barry Hayles was delivered to Louis the First on a plate. A drop of the shoulder, swivel and the ball was drilled low into the corner of the net at an empty Hammersmith End.

Normally the goal would have been noisily celebrated by that quarter of the ground. But the rules had been changed. To coin a phrase, the goalposts had been moved. It was different. A gaping, cavernous expanse of unoccupied terrace. This was Europe. At times, a contradiction in terms.

UEFA Intertoto Cup, third round, first leg.
Venue: Craven Cottage. *Attendance:* 5,199.

FULHAM (0) 1   AIGALEO (0) 0
Fulham: Van der Sar, Ouaddou (Legwinski 45), Harley, Knight, Goma, Malbranque (Hayles 66), Marlet, Davis, Sava (Saha 45), Collins (captain), Boa Morte. Unused subs: Herrera, Melville, Goldbaek, Stolcers.
Aigaleo: Cidibe, Papoutsis, Meidanis, Alexopoulos, Chatsis (Antonetti 69), Edusei, Stefanov (Wanga 52), Skopelitis (captain), Christou, Fotakis, Chloros (Agritis 61). Unused subs: Kottaras, Psomas, Makris, Simeonidis.
Scorer: Saha 78.
Bookings: Meidanis, Alexopoulos, Wanga.
Referee: J. Ver Eecke (Belgium). *Assistants:* M. Simons, L. Rems (Belgium).

A near stalemate of a contest that will go down in history in the memories of the faithful. And, because of the result, we harboured high hopes for our flying visit to the Hellenes a week later. All we had to do was keep our nerve. Stiff upper lip an' all that…

2: GOIN' DUTCH

Kí Klaksvik v Fulham Ladies – Tuesday, 19th August 2003

A whole new experience was beckoning. Fulham Ladies' entry into the UEFA Women's Cup presented an opportunity to examine yet another facet of the beautiful game. The group stage of the third round of the competition had pitched our girls into action with hosts from the Netherlands, plus opponents from the Faroe Islands and Moldova. Intriguing enough for yours truly to get off his ever-spreading boompsadaisy and give it a go.

Another aspect to be taken into consideration was that the venues to be visited promised to be out of the ordinary from the norm. Potentially off the well-trodden masculine European footballing circuit. Ripe for exploration. In the event, the inaugural venture out to Sassenheim, near the coastal resort of Nordwijk-an-Zee, was a real eye-opener. It provided me with a whole new insight into the behind the scenes workings of ladies' football. Other than being an education, it was a whole lot of fun as well.

Being adopted by the squad as a sort of unofficial technical advisor was a bonus. It meant that I became involved in training sessions and could also attend the UEFA committee meetings, albeit with a watching brief. That in itself was a whole new ball game. Aside from that there were a couple of amusing incidents that deserve setting down in print. Firstly there was the business of an ornithological DNA test and the consequences of. Secondly, and more personally, there was the instance where a training ball was hoofed into an adjacent canal. Your oft scribbling factotum was saved the indignity of stripping to the buff by a timely intervention. Whilst one pondered the meaning of life, two of the livelier squad members commandeered a rowing boat to retrieve the spherical object from a watery grave. Sighs of relief all round. It could have proved so mightily embarrassing. "Wotcha cock" would not have proved a particularly apt expression at that time.

Just to add insult to injury, the boat possessed neither oars nor rowlocks… All this and the tournament hadn't even started. Our opponents for the opening encounter were Klaksvik, from the Faroese island of Bordoy. On an outside pitch next to the main stadium, Fulham started brightly. Before too long they had assumed virtually total control, knocking the ball about with verve and flair. Indeed, there were stages toward the latter end of the first half which saw them permanently encamped in their opponents' half of the field. Meaningful possession at its most effective. Nil-four at the interval was doubled by the final whistle. The gallant Klaksvik girls had become almost overrun at the death, such was the Fulham

UEFA Women's Cup

Programmaboekje
2003/'04

Deelnemers:

FC Cordu Anenii Noi
Ki Klaksvik
Fulham Ladies FC
v.v. Ter Leede

Group 8 tournament programme. Dyslexia rules? Note the spelling of 'FC Codru'.

superiority. It was an impressive start in the European arena which augured well for the two remaining matches.

UEFA Women's Cup, third round, group 8.
Venue: Sportpark de 'Roodemolen'. *Attendance:* 38.

KÍ KLAKSVIK (0) 0   FULHAM LADIES (4) 8
Klaksvik: V. Andreasen, J. Sirdal, R. Andreasen (captain), M. Josephsen, R.B. Andreasen, A. Justesen, P. Mikkelsen (Paula Sjostein 84), V. Bjartald (Petra Sjostein 84), U. Olsen, E. Simonsen (A. Olsen 71), B. Skaala. Unused subs: M. Vid Neyst, A. Sjostein, M. Joensen.
Fulham: S. Chamberlain, K. Jerray-Silver, C. Yorston, J. Wright, M. Phillip (captain) (M. Hickmott 49), K. Chapman, R. McArthur, R. Unitt, R. Yankey, S. Duncan (T. Waine 58), G. Ritchie (D. Bird 80). Unused subs: H. Cox, S. Flint, C. White, R. Bennett.
Scorers: Yankey 7, Chapman 23, 35, Yorston 29, Duncan 57, Waine 69, 86, Jerray-Silver 79.
Referee: K. Elovirta (Finland).

Experience shows that life never ceases to amaze. Likewise, never let it be said that females are the weaker sex, especially when it comes down to organising themselves to play football. Klaksvik's travel arrangements were a case in point. Their convoluted passage involved an initial boat trip from the island of Bordoy to Tórshavn, the capital. Following were two flights, Tórshavn–Copenhagen and then Copenhagen–Amsterdam. Thence by coach to the destination. The total cost of the venture was in the region of fifteen thousand pounds, all of which was raised by the girls themselves. Admirable. There are times when us blokes just have to hold up our hands to them. And say "well done". Such is the lure of European football.

UEFA Women's Cup 2003-04, third round composition:

Group 1
Brondby IF (Denmark) - *hosts*
FK Mašinac-Classic Niš (Serbia & Montenegro)
Kilmarnock (Scotland)
KR Reykjavik (Iceland)

Group 2
FC Bobruichanka (Belarus) - *hosts*

FC Schwerzenbach (Switzerland)
Gömrükçü Baku (Azerbaijan)
AE Aegina (Greece)

Group 3
Umeå IK (Sweden) - *hosts*
SK Slavia Praha (Czech Republic)
Newtonabbey Strikers WFC (Northern Ireland)
FC Clujana Cluj (Romania)

Group 4
FC Energy Voronezh (Russia) - *hosts*
FC Foroni Verona (Italy)
1. FC Femina Budapest (Hungary)
NK Osijek (Croatia)

Group 5
Legend - Checksil (Ukraine) - *hosts*
Malmö FF (Sweden)
FC United Jakobstad Pietarsaari (Finland)
Maccabi Holon FC (Israel)

Group 6
Kolbotn IL 1 (Norway) - *hosts*
Juvisy FCF (France)
KS AZS Wroclaw (Poland)
UCD Women's Football Club (Eire)

Group 7
Athletic Club 2 (Spain) - *hosts*
1. FFC Frankfurt (Germany)
S União 1° Dez.3 (Portugal)
SV Neulengbach (Austria)

Group 8
VV Ter Leede (Holland) - *hosts*
Fulham Ladies (England)
Kí Klaksvik (Faroe Islands)
FC Codru Anenii Noi (Moldova)

3: COTTAGE CRUMBS

Fulham v Bologna – Wednesday, 2nd May 1973

The final edible footballing portion from a platter, already three quarters digested. Coffee and biscuits to follow. Most modern day aficionados of the black and white are able to identify Bologna as the vanquished opponents in the 2002 Intertoto Cup Final. Some with longer memories may recall the fixture that this chapter relates to. Yet, as an interesting aside, when was the first time that Fulham appeared in the Stadio Renato Dall'Ara? Oh yes, and twice within a week. The mid seventies era saw our first team gain a creditable 1–1 draw against Bologna in a friendly fixture, John Mitchell being the scorer. Two days later our stiffs were soundly

Anglo Italian Tournament

FULHAM
v
BOLOGNA

Wednesday 2nd May 1973
Kick off 7.45 p.m.

Official Programme Price 3p

beaten 3–0 by Zenit Leningrad, now St. Petersburg. Proof that the long term memory is still functioning.

Return, if you will, to our original tale. The Bologna encounter that we are focussing on came right at the stub end of the 72–73 season. The fourth of four from the club's only excursion into the Anglo-Italian Tournament. No other first team games were programmed to be played at the ancestral home until the coming of the new campaign. A long, hot summer lay ahead. Regrettably, the attendance that long ago May evening reflected the fact. Only the diehards bothered to come along and offer support. The malaise of low tournament gates was not just indicative of England either. Yet there was still a game to be watched and statistics to be garnered. Thirty years later the information could form part of the cornerstone of the club's fledgling European archive material.

Our Italian opponents, a club rich in tradition, were expected to be a difficult nut to crack. Even though Fulham were off to a flier, a Jimmy Conway effort hitting the net after only six minutes, the Rossoblu continued to provide stiff opposition. They became almost impossible to break down, forming an im-penetrable barrier in front of custodian Pietro Battara. Overcoming the intricacies of catenaccio was still proving to be a difficult exercise, even with the benefit of having played three games in the competition up to that point.

With Fulham still one ahead at the interval, Bologna revised their tactics, changing their shape for the second half with the addition of a substitute, Vieri, in the forward line. In doing so, they moved out of their defensive shell and went on the attack. The change took all of eleven minutes to bear fruit when Vieri equalised. The status quo achieved, they reverted to type. All quiet on the Apennine front.

The stalemate situation was not exactly helped by having Italian match officials present. It is not sour grapes but the referee did appear to condone some of the blatant time-wasting employed by the visitors in the later stages of the game. Competition rules stated that Italian refereeing teams should officiate in England and vice versa. So best get on with it. Even if it meant Paul Went collecting a yellow card for querying a decision in the referee's native language. Linguistic skills could also be a disadvantage too.

Anglo Italian Tournament, group 2.
Venue: Craven Cottage. *Attendance:* 3,836.

FULHAM (1) 1 BOLOGNA (0) 1
Fulham: Webster, Cutbush, Moreline, Mullery (captain), Went, Horne, Jimmy Conway, Earle, Carlton, Lloyd, Barrett. Unused subs: Mitchell, Lacy, Strong.
Bologna: Battara, Roversi, Fedele, Caporale, Cresci, Gregori, Perani (Vieri 45), Ghetti, Savoldi, Bulgarelli, Novellini.

Scorers: Jimmy Conway 6, Vieri 56.
Booking: Went.
Referee: Renzo Torelli. *Linesmen:* A. Patroncini, F. Schiaffino.

Purely for the sake of nostalgia, other results from that evening and a group table are included here for comparison. As can be seen, Fulham never really got to grips with the Italian defensive systems that were prevalent at the time. They finished with four draws. It was to be another twenty-nine years before the club would appear in recognised European competition again.

GROUP 1:
Verona v Manchester United   1–4
Bari v Hull City   Unknown
Lazio v Luton Town   2–2
Fiorentina v Crystal Palace   2–2

GROUP 2
Fulham v Bologna   1–1
Newcastle United v Torino   5–1
Oxford United v Como   1–0
Blackpool v Roma   2–1

GROUP 2 FINAL TABLE

	P	W	D	L	F	A	Pts
Newcastle United	4	4	0	0	10	1	8
Blackpool	4	4	0	0	7	1	8
Oxford United	4	2	2	0	4	1	6
Fulham	4	0	4	0	3	3	4
Torino	4	0	2	2	3	8	2
Bologna	4	0	2	2	2	6	2
Roma	4	0	1	3	2	7	1
Como	4	0	1	3	0	6	1

A final tasty morsel to assuage the appetite. There were a sextet of other players who were associated with Fulham Football Club at one time or another who also appeared in the tournament. They were Don Shanks, Alan Slough, Viv Busby and John Ryan, all of Luton Town plus Dave Roberts and John Evanson of Oxford United. If memory serves me right, Newcastle United and Fiorentina contested the final. Yet for the life of me, I cannot remember the ultimate winners. Any suggestions before I reach for the dyspepsia tablets.

4: POST HORS D'OEUVRES

HNK Hajduk Split v Fulham – Thursday 19th September 2002

Please permit me to continue in a culinary vein for a little while yet. At least for this chapter… With both gastronomic and footballing senses already titillated by a four dish appetiser, more was awaited with relish. Further components to the main course of a potential continental feast. Hot and spicy. Just the way I like it. A Dalmatian adventure, rich in promise, was the prize as Hajduk Split were paired with us from the Monégasque pot.

Fulham's inaugural UEFA Cup opponents opened up the memory bank of yours truly. Visions of a seventies era family holiday to the former Yugoslavia came flooding back. A reminder of the Istrian Peninsula to the north. Happily, still part of the modern day Croatia. Outdoor grill bars amid the pine trees. Chilling out beneath the stars with a loved one. Plus a bottle of rich ruby local wine. Cevapcici, svenska but or rajnici. The regional dishes of meat balls, half a chicken or kebabs have got me drooling. Proof that the romance of it has not been extinguished. If one then introduced the Fulham European factor to the concoction and gave it a stir it became simply irresistible. Bursting with flavour. An Adriatic treat.

Which is the prime reason why your scribe elected to make his own way once again. Not for me a twenty-four hours supporters' charter. In and out on a day trip was felt to be a tad too regimented for this free spirit. Four nights away looked to be sufficient time to rediscover the magic of the region. Partake of some of the culture, assimilate the local vibes from a World Heritage site and enjoy another classic Lilliewhite performance. Top banana. A restorative for the soul. Another example of the magic of Fulham.

Not that the trip was all about lazy days or foolish aspirations. Our UEFA baptism looked like providing the sternest test yet. Over the years, HNK had accumulated a proud European pedigree, particularly on home soil. The Torcida, 'the torch' of their Poljud Stadium, manifested a fearsome reputation which was not for the faint-hearted. From memory, our hosts' jousts with English clubs reached back as far as Spurs' 'glory, glory' days in the late sixties when they met in the Cup Winners Cup. In their heyday Hajduk would have provided a severe obstacle to Fulham. Years of strife in the Balkans had a detrimental effect on the fortunes of many of the established club sides in the former Yugoslavia. Therefore, it was felt that if everything remained equal, Fulham had a more than even chance of progression.

The one thing that can be assured about football watching in this neck of the woods is that it is guaranteed to become lively. Not exactly sweetness and light but full of incident nonetheless. The Slavic temperament coming to the fore, one suspects. The actions of the Torcida could therefore be construed as being intimidatory towards the unwary. No exceptions were made for the coming of Fulham. A huge banner stating 'CA JE PUSTA LONDRA KONTRA SPLITU GRADU' stretched across the entire width of the home end. 'You have your London but we have our Split' we were told. Lines from a one hundred year old operetta. Open to interpretation, when put in a footballing context, yet hardly conducive to an act of friendship. Around here philosophies such as that came with the territory. More menacing though was the banner that read 'TORCIDA DUCÉ'. It came with an accompanying image of Mussolini giving a fascist salute. Bang out of order. We were guests so it had to be tolerated, sickeningly provocative though it may have been.

The script had been prepared and punctuated. A cauldron of noise, flares and smoke that first invaded then scrambled the senses. Quite damaging to the mental equilibrium. 256 Lilliewhite stalwarts gave of their best in engineering support, straining limb, sinew and larynx in an attempt to be heard above the din. For the first twenty minutes Hajduk hit Fulham with pace down the flanks, whipping in some searching and very dangerous crosses. Our rearguard held firm. The attacks were negated coolly and calmly. The only real incident of the opening half came when Edwin Van der Sar was forced to make a double reflex save. Aided and abetted by the woodwork, he denied Dario Srna, the pick of the home forwards, after twenty-nine minutes. Reference should also be made to the performance of Barry Hayles up front. Buffeted and manhandled throughout the duration, he nevertheless persevered, just getting on with playing his normal game. As a battering ram he was peerless.

The interval came with the contest still finely balanced at level pegging. Intuition was telling me that we would still get a result. The original assessment was on track. Hajduk appeared to have all but blown themselves out. All we had to do was to take the game to them. And when, on fifty minutes, the moment of glory came, all hell broke loose in the visitors' block. Steed Malbranque galloped clear for a one-on-one with the keeper. No contest. Nil-one Fulham! Grown men wept, kissed, hugged each other. Pinched their neighbour to ensure that it wasn't a dream. Such were the feelings of elation that your scribe almost suffered a misdemeanour of the nether regions. But not quite. Indescribable. We were flying. And then some.

The remaining forty minutes absolutely whizzed by. There were firemen on the pitch dealing with flares hurled there by disgruntled locals. One defensive scare near the end. Easily dealt with. Final whistle and it was all over. Exhilaration.

1. PLETIKOSA, STIPE (GK) (cap.)
6. ÐOLONGA, VLATKO
7. VEJIĆ, HRVOJE
10. CAREVIĆ, MARIO
11. DERANJA, ZVONIMIR
14. ANDRIĆ, SRÐAN
17. VUKOVIĆ, HRVOJE
18. SRNA, DARIO
20. RAČUNICA, DEAN
21. MILADIN, DARKO
23. NERETLJAK, MATO

25. RUNJE, ZLATKO (GK)
2. BUTOROVIĆ, DARKO
3. PIRIĆ, IVICA
4. RADELJIĆ, IVAN
8. BULE, NINO
15. BRGLES, DARIO
24. GUDELJ, HRVATIN

TRENER: VULIĆ, ZORAN

REFEREES:

FERNANDO CARMONA MENDEZ (SPAIN)

RAFAEL GUERRERO ALONSO (SPAIN)
JULIAN GONZALEZ RAYO (SPAIN)

ALFONSO PINO ZAMORANO (SPAIN)

DELEGATE:

MEHMED SPAHO (BiH)

1. VAN DER SAR, EDWIN (GK)
3. BREVETT, RUFUS
4. MELVILLE, ANDY (cap.)
6. INAMOTO, JUNICHI
7. MARLET, STEVE
14. MALBRANQUE, STEED
15. HAYLES, BARRY
18. LEGWINSKI, SYLVAIN
23. DAVIS, SEAN
24. GOMA, ALAIN
25. OUADDOU, ABDES

12. TAYLOR, MAIK (GK)
8. CLARK, LEE
9. SAVA, FACUNDO
10. COLLINS, JOHN
16. KNIGHT, ZAT
27. WOME, PIERRE
40. STOLCERS ANDY

TRENER: TIGANA, JEAN

Teamsheet. This copy was retrieved from the home dressing room. Note the HNK coach's substitution scribblings.

Postcard showing aerial view of the Poljud Stadium The 'Torcida' gathered behind the near end goal.

Advertisement showing ticket prices in Croatian Kunar.

Heads high yet hearts pumping. Knocked Intertoto Bologna into a cocked hat. Wait around for what seemed an eternity. Day trip coaches depart for Kasteli Airport. Incognito, we try to blend into the blackness of an Adriatic night on our way back to the seafront. My beach-side apartment at Podstrana was still another eight kilometres distant… The first course had been easily consumed without ever needing antacid remedies. Aside from the less than savoury sauces, it had been most piquant on the palate.

UEFA Cup, first round, first leg.
Venue: Poljud Stadion. *Attendance:* 33,000.

HNK HAJDUK SPLIT (0) 0   FULHAM (0) 1
Hajduk: Pletikosa (captain), Dolonga, Vejic, Carevic, Deranja, Andric, Vukovic (Piric 85), Srna (Brgles 84), Racunica (Bule 69), Miladin, Neretljak. Unused subs: Runje, Butorovic, Radeljic, Gudelj.
Fulham: Van der Sar, Brevett (Wome 63), Melville (captain), Inamoto (Clark 78), Marlet (Sava 84), Malbranque, Hayles, Legwinski, Davis, Goma, Ouaddou. Unused subs: Taylor, Knight, Collins, Stolcers.
Scorer: Malbranque 50.
Bookings: Carevic, Miladin.
Referee: F.C. Mendez (Spain). *Assistants:* R.G. Alonso, J.G. Rayo (Spain).

In closing, special mention must be made of the most convoluted independent sortie yet. Flight to Bologna, train to Trieste, local charabanc through Slovenia and on to Rijeka then maritime ferry down. Forty-eight hours one way. A top effort. Others flew to Trieste and drove down in hire cars or took the ferry across the Adriatic from Ancona to Split or Zadar. The various travel itineraries are becoming interesting too. Further proof, if proof were needed, that the trailblazers of 2002 are just as adventurous as their peers.

5: ROLL OVER

FC Codru Anenii Noi v Fulham Ladies – Thursday, 21st August 2003

Moldova. Not a musical interlude for honky tonk joanna but a Women's UEFA Cup tie. A footballing oddity which, at times, beggared description. In retrospect, there were elements surrounding this sporting get together that bordered on the unreal. Tales of the unexpected might be seen as more appropriate.

First, there was the vexing question regarding the origin of Fulham Ladies' opponents. Being of an enquiring nature, I wasn't at all sure about the location of FC Codru Anenii Noi within what was formerly the Soviet Socialist Republic of Moldavskaya. It took a fair amount of research to pinpoint the town of Anenii Noi as being approximately 25 kilometres east of Chisinau, the capital. On the road to Tiraspol, the second city. In the expansion of knowledge therefore, nothing ventured, nothing gained.

Furthermore, it had taken the Moldovan party some 54 hours to arrive in the Rijnland for the tournament. Overland by motor coach. One driver. No obvious Health & Safety restrictions. Other than that, the opposition were largely an unknown quantity. Yet, back to unreality… With Ter Leede, the hosts, taking their turn on the outside pitch, it was Fulham's opening appearance in the main stadium. Performing in front of a pitifully small gathering of some thirty souls. And, believe this if you will, I was asked to stand by as a potential stretcher bearer. Luminous jacket and all. In addition, that is, to my other duties of technical advisor, match statistician, reporter, general factotum and chief cheerleader in a support group of four persons.

Watching women's football abroad certainly does get one involved. Allied to the Moldovan's excitable Latin temperament and their apparent innate ability to throw themselves on to the floor and feign dead at the merest collision with a blade of grass meant that my services could have been needed. On several occasions there I was, awaiting at the starting blocks with a trusty stretcher. All to no avail. Just who would have assisted in carrying the other end had the situation arisen, lord alone knows.

FC Codru's game plan was obvious in its transparency. Straight from the kick-off they retreated into regimented ranks of grim defence. Their disciplined back line, whose sole function was to frustrate, had to be firstly negated, then overcome, and finally overwhelmed. It took Fulham nearly half an hour to find a way through. After going one down Codru just capitulated. And, dare one say it, rolled over. Our girls' initial patience, skilful probing and persistence had been

Ter Leede club magazine covering men's, ladies', and junior football.

justly rewarded. Altogether nine Lilliewhite goals were registered and in some style. Almost at will in the end.

***Women's UEFA Cup, third round, group 8**.*
Venue: Sportpark de 'Roodemolen'. *Attendance:* 30.

FC CODRU ANENII NOI (0) 1   FULHAM LADIES (4) 9
FC Codru: L. Pop, V. Ilin, C. Dolgovici, A. Toma, V. Rusu, D. Pufulete (captain), O. Sava, O. Tanschi, I. Deliu, M. Ciurdas, L. Leu. Unused subs: E. Pavalachi, P. Capcanari, I. Budestean.

Fulham: S. Chamberlain, K. Jerray-Silver, C. Yorston (R. Bennett 78), M. Phillip (captain), K. Chapman, R. McArthur, R. Unitt, T. Waine, M. Hickmott, R. Yankey (S. Flint 49), G. Ritchie (C. White 47). Unused subs: H. Cox, J. Wright, S. Duncan, D. Bird.
Scorers: Chapman 26, Waine 38, 50, 84, Yankey 42, Hickmott 43, Pufulete 62, McArthur 71 (pen), Jerray-Silver 77, Flint 81.
Bookings: Jerray-Silver, Toma.
Referee: R. Ruiz Tadaronte (Spain).

In the final analysis I could not see a valid reason for the Moldovan's tactics. To travel over three quarters of the width of the European continent with such limited ambition just seemed curious to me. I couldn't get my head round it, to use a modern expression. Their outlook meant that they were beaten before they started. The eight goal drubbing just accentuated the point.

A souvenir from Ter Leede—the twenty-five year history of the Dutch hosts.

6: CHANGE OF ADDRESS

Fulham v FC Sochaux-Montbeliard – Wednesday, 31st July 2002

From SW6 6HH to W12 7PA. What's in an amendment to a postcode? Quite a lot, actually. As a dyed-in-the-wool Hammersmith Ender of long standing, an enforced relocation to what was previously deemed to be alien territory is a wee bit hard to swallow. From the ambience of the bright sunshine that had bathed Craven Cottage for the apparent swansong to a torrential downpour of monsoonal proportions that enveloped our temporary quarters on the White City estate. Even the elements were conspiring against us.

Not the time for comparisons either. It was the same competition. Just a different round. For a European semi-final, there was a pitifully small crowd in attendance. Whether it was the inclement conditions or as a result of the move inland from the river was not for discussion. Tigana's troops had a fixture to be won. A first leg result to be attained. No whingeing or moaning. Best get on with it.

Fulham appeared to be having the rub of the green in terms of the draw. For the third time on the spin in the competition, they had been drawn at home in the first leg. To maximise that advantage, they needed to produce a positive result to take away from home. Unlike the already vanquished Haka and Aigaleo, Sochaux presented an entirely different proposition. Hailing from the Doubs region of eastern France, close to the Swiss border, both visitors and hosts had already locked horns in a friendly fixture. A match amicale in the Stade Bonal some eight months previously had resulted in a 2–0 home win. Sochaux were also well known for their almost unceasing production line of talented young players emerging into the professional ranks. Such background knowledge suggested an evenly balanced tie.

Indeed, so delicate was the symmetry between the two teams that a decisive goal was netted only seconds from the end of time added on. More of that later... Fulham wrested command directly from the kick-off but their all-action passing game became hampered by both the damp conditions and eerie atmospherics. Sylvain Legwinski's header thudded against the bar after thirteen minutes as Fulham attempted to assert their authority on the game. Sochaux were not to be denied and only the long legs of Edwin Van der Sar saved a goal-bound attempt by the Brazilian, dos Santos Silva.

The goalless half-time stalemate was brightened by the introduction of debutant Junichi Inamoto, on loan from Gamba Osaka via Arsenal reserves. The addition of the attacking midfield player became the catalyst of the production of

FULHAM

Your Official Fulham FC Matchday Programme **£1.00**

FULHAM versus SOCHAUX
Wednesday 31st July 2002 Kick Off 7.45 pm
Intertoto Cup Semi Final 1st Leg

INTERTOTO CUP

adidas
Kit Sponsor

betfair
Mens Team Sponsor

more and more Lilliewhite pressure. Until the final minute of injury time when Sean Davis unleashed a left-footer high into the Sochaux net. Direct from an Inamoto corner. First impressions of the Japanese World Cup star? Priceless. In whatever currency. Monetary or otherwise.

UEFA Intertoto Cup, semi-final, first leg.
Venue: Loftus Road. *Attendance:* 4,717.

FULHAM (0) 1   FC SOCHAUX-MONTBELIARD (0) 0
Fulham: Van der Sar, Ouaddou (Knight 63), Brevett, Melville (captain), Goma, Legwinski (Inamoto 45), Marlet, Malbranque (Hayles 69), Saha, Davis, Boa Morte. Unused subs: Collins, Herrera, Harley, Sava.
Sochaux: Richert, Flachez (captain), Saveljic, Lonfat (Chedli 86), Boudarene, Frau (Zairi 12), dos Santos Silva (de Carvalho 75), Pedretti, Raschke, Monsoreau, Mathieu. Unused subs: Daguet, Tall, Isabey, Daf.
Scorer: Davis 90.
Bookings: Marlet, Davis, Richert, Saveljic.
Referee: S. Corpodean (Romania). *Assistants:* I. Muresan, M. Savaniu (Romania).

The trip to France a week hence now looks interesting. My own feeling is that there are more goals in the tie. Plus, a European final is beckoning. Que sera, sera. Come on, you Whites.

7: TRAILBLAZING

Torino v Fulham – Wednesday, 4th April 1973

Torneo fashion. And in fine style for the day too. Our second foray towards the Piemonte region in the lee of the Alps came at the beginning of April 1973. No fool's errand either. Quite the opposite. As had been the case to Como some weeks before, the majority of our happy band of West London pathfinders travelled overland to Turin by rail. On a club trip, several dozen strong. Rather than the handful that ventured out to the Italian lakes.

Despite the retelling of the tale over three decades later, there are still visual flashes that both come to the fore and require description. Moments of wayfaring bliss. The first instance was very much a 'believe this if you will' moment. The Folkestone–Calais ferry that conveyed us across the Channel contained much the same crew members who had hosted us en route to Como. So having already established a good working rapport with the bar staff, the outcome was that we arrived on the dockside at Calais Maritime in a really jolly mood. With plenty of supplies to sustain us ahead of many hours of chemin de fer passage.

Then there was the affair of the young Irish girl who was journeying on her own. Who immediately gained a goodly number of male friends among the Fulham folk. Gentlemen all, it should be stated. Except that there were some very puzzled looks when she tripped off down the platform at Torino PN saying that her sole reason in voyaging so far from Erin was to become a nun. But there again, you meet all sorts…

The warmth of the early morning sunshine plus the anticipation of a nourishing repast had put a seasonal spring in our step. Breakfast, Italian style amongst the

The match tickets. The 'Biglietto Di Invito' was a complimentary.

colonnades along Corso Vittorio Emanuelle II, adjacent to the station at Porta Nuova, was a letdown. Certainly a disappointment for those not au fait with local cuisine. By no means could tosti and cappuccino compare with the delights of a full English. All it could do was to temporarily fill the hole.

Next on the agenda was a visit to the stadium and an exploratory look-around. As you do. A short but novel experience, a ride on a tram brought us to the environs of the Stadio Comunale. Our mission—to reconnoitre the area ahead of the arrival of the main party of supporters—was peremptorily curtailed by some subterranean noises caused by emergent pangs of hunger. What to do? Adjourn to a convenient pavement café and stock up on some filling cheese and salami rolls. And birra. Several birras in fact.

Followed by several more. Until the bladder gave up the ghost and a visit to the boys room was called for. The establishment that we were frequenting had the relevant facilities situated inside and down the stairs. In the basement. Across a large and dingy room. Which contained a circular table, covered in green baize. Which, at first glance, appeared to be surrounded by a group of local males playing cards. Except that, to a man, they were all dressed the same. Sharp suits, dark coats and sunglasses. Get the picture.

They became more agitated by the minute as an almost continuous procession of Hammersmith Enders came traipsing by looking for the hole in the floor in which to relieve themselves. So much so that after an hour or so suffering endless interruptions, their patience finally gave out. The departed in a fleet of limousines, casting what one took to be envious glances in our direction. At a party still in full swing. Looking back now, the suspicion is that it was a first introduction to the mob for most of us. I shall leave you to conclude who looked to have made the most impression.

A good omen perchance. So, with the sun having reaching its zenith in the heavens, we crossed the road to enter the huge concrete bowl that was the Stadio Comunale. Even with only ten thousand present in a capacity of seventy-one thousand, the atmosphere was stifling. And the noise! A timpani section on the home terrace that consisted of the whole range of drums. Base, kettle and side. The works. And all being bashed unmercifully in support of their favourites, Not good, especially in my case where a swift siesta might have been more appropriate. Never let it be said that Fulham supporters don't rise to a challenge. We got on with noisily giving backing to the mighty Lilliewhites, cranking the volume up still further. A small knot of English adventurers versus the Turin Sinfonia. Yet, as the game progressed, the clamour from the Italians reduced suddenly. To nothingness.

It had something to do with Fulham's opening goal, right on the stroke of half-time. Leaving us whooping and screaming with delight. Press reports described

QUI SONO IN VENDITA I BIGLIETTI PER LA GARA
TORINO - FULHAM

TIPOGRAFIA ARTALE - TORINO TEL. 542.001

Above: poster advertising a match ticket sales point. Also available was the following week's fixture—a European Cup tie between Juventus and Derby County. Below: the traditional postcard home, and a cluster of West London pathfinders in the stadium.

TORINO DALL' AEREO - IL VALENTINO E FIUME PO

the strike as 'a superb diving header from Les Strong.' Yet there was more to it than that. Much more. The construction of the move was something special. The ball was moved down the pitch with such fluency that Torino didn't even get a sniff. A pinpoint cross and…Strongie, bless him, was merely the executioner. Oh what joy!

A jovial half-time passed all too quickly and we returned to the business at hand. Helping the team hold on to their hard won lead. Which was achieved, up until four minutes from the final whistle. Then the defence appeared to suffer a rush of blood. Leaving Claudio Sala with the easiest of opportunities to equalise. So near… But an encouraging result nonetheless.

Anglo-Italian Tournament, group 2.
Venue: Stadio Comunale. *Attendance:* 10,000 approx.

TORINO (0) 1 FULHAM (1) 1
Torino: Castellini, Lombardo, Mozzini, Zecchini, Cereser, Fossati (Masiello 69), Rampanti, Ferrini (Madde 45), Bui, Sala, Pulici. Unused subs: Sattolo, Novellini, Bortot.
Fulham: Mellor, Cutbush, Callaghan, Mullery (captain), Went, Horne, Strong, Mitchell, Earle, Pinkney (Lloyd 53), Barrett. Unused subs: Webster, Shrubb, Fraser.
Scorers: Strong 44, Sala 86.
Referee: B. James (South Croydon).

Off we marched with heads held high. There was still one task to be dealt with before we could go home. Security. As has been said before, collectively the Cottage faithful beyond these shores are not there to be taken liberties with. Blackpool, the previous tournament visitors had their team coach damaged after the game. The same fate was not going to befall Fulham. Not if we could help it. So when the Torino tifosi arrived outside the players' entrance, hell bent on mischief, their way was barred. True to form, they about faced and high tailed it out of there. When the Fulham players emerged, freshly scrubbed, to meet their adoring travelling public, they were totally unaware that anything had ever been amiss. Sorted.

The Turin Sinfonia.

8: THE LIFE OF RILEY

Hertha BSC, Berlin v Fulham – Tuesday, 26th November 2002

The good times just keep rolling along. Like the Thames but without the resonance of a gravelly voice. Subliminal that, the adjacency to Craven Cottage. Yet one digresses… For an ageing soul, driven by incessant wanderlust, what had gone before were seen as merely tasters. Enough to whet the appetite. Aperitifs in the grand scheme of things. The 'Oldham' of the Finnish lakes, the 'pits' of the Hellenes, the rain in Saone falling mainly on the…, citta della cultura, coastal Dalmacija and blues by triple. All had been interesting and educational.

When the Berlin plum was thumbed from la titfer Nyonnaise it was the answer to many personal aspirations. A profusion of options cultural, architectural and historical offered themselves as open to inspection. Yours truly would be in his element. The UEFA Cup fixture between Hertha BSC and those glorious Lilliewhites would be an important, though additional, bonus. The icing on the cake.

One hadn't spent much time there since the European Championships of 1988, overnighting in the Western sector for a Michael Jackson concert. There had been sufficient spare time for an inebriated stagger along the Unter Den Linden. Through the Wall via Checkpoint Charlie. Then, in 1993, a coach excursion through the now unified city en route from Katowice to Oslo. One really couldn't tell which side of the former divide we were on, except for an unscheduled interruption at Schoenefeld Airport, twenty kilometres to the east.

That's torn it… A futile atempt to keep the ticket pristine.

For one with an enquiring mind there was much to investigate. Letting the imagination run riot could almost herald a field day. Spandau, whether for the prison remains or the ballet. True. The Reichstag, in a search for the missing testicle. Check out Kurfurstendamm and the Hard Rock Café. The plastic was guaranteed to take a hammering. The Zoologische Garten, Alexanderplatz,

Potsdam. Endless variations on a theme. More than enough in which to immerse oneself for two or three days.

Fulham, as us older devotees should recall, had competed in the Olympia Stadion before. Finishing up as winners too. Saturday 5 August 1967 saw us defeat Tennis Borussia West Berlin 4-1 by virtue of a goal from Fred Callaghan and a hat trick from Allan Clarke. For the statisticians among you the line up that day was Macedo, Mealand, Brown, Ryan, Nichols, Jimmy Conway, Haynes, Callaghan, Earle (Dyson), Clarke and Barrett. Even though the game had been played thirty-five years before, if one was looking for positives that result augured well.

In a more personal sense, a more congenial prospect appeared. A most pleasant surprise in fact. A lady travelling companion offered to accompany your scribe on the journey. Although the situation meant curtailment of any of the more dubious nocturnal activities one could more than live with it. Thus the offer was graciously accepted. It doesn't get any better than that.

At the time of writing, our hosts' sixth place in the Bundesliga intimated that they were quality opposition. Yet Fulham's performances in Europe this season, where they had both persevered and played attractive football, left one feeling that they were in with more than a shout. Even the pre-match electronic messages that were emanating from the German capital were of a conciliatory nature. Quite the opposite to the hostile and downright aggressive drivel that had come out of Zagreb. Although it made a pleasant change, experience told to wait and see. The proof of the pudding and all that.

As for the kick-off time being adjusted to meet the avaricious demands of German television, from a travelling fan's point of view it was of little consequence. If the venue was to have been the dark side of the moon, with a three in the morning commencement and it involved Fulham… Us Hammersmith End folks would find the means to be present. Simple. Nothing else matters.

Dienstag therefore became the focus of our attention. With the destination being so accessible the numbers of day-tripping intrepids had swelled the ranks of the Lilliewhite faithful to close on a thousand. Closeted in a block adjacent to the refurbishment works, alongside a huge crane and cheek by jowl with a couple of monster inflatables, the atmosphere was initially rather surreal. Strange to say the least. But it got better as more and more Fulham arrived and laid their flags. The provision of vocal support was our mission so we just got on with it. Cheerfully and lustily. Such was the volume that the locals will remember the efforts of the choristers of SW6 for a long time to come. Strains of the delightful "We've got Melvinho" drifting away on the evening air through the Berliner Wald was a sound to behold. An act of togetherness with the skipper.

But enough of the preliminaries. The opening quarter was low key. Much checking out of defences. Sparring contained within the middle of the park. Yawn

HERTHANER

Stadionmagazin

SAISON 2002 2003

Offizielles Stadionmagazin von Hertha BSC
Dienstag, 26.11.2002
1,– Euro

Heft 3

www.herthabsc.de

playberlin

UEFA CUP   3. Runde · Bei uns zu Gast: FC Fulham

inducing if our European Tour merchants hadn't been so voluble. The local pilsener had a lot to answer for. Yet, at this level, one mistake means a high price is paid. A second's loss of concentration at the back allowed Stefan Beinlich, once of Aston Villa, to open the scoring on twenty-eight minutes with a free header.

Or as near as damnit. The goal had an immediate effect on the gallery. Amongst the faithful it both energised and raised the noise levels still further. There was a method in our apparent madness. The singing acts as a concealment for a change

Match poster.

of strategy. At that stage our problem seemed to be lack of width, brought about in the main by the continual compression of play. A half-time substitution overcame the difficulty at a stroke. Luis Boa Morte was introduced to the stage to perform. Both offensively and defensively, in his own inimitable manner.

Immediate expansiveness. Fulham swept on to the front foot and had Hertha rocking. All over the shop. Attack in triplicate. Parity came in eight minutes. A Martin Djetou effort hit the post leaving 'Bob' Marlet to knock home into an unguarded net. Oh yes! Have some of that. The feeling is indescribable. Everything else pales into insignificance. It justifies going the distance. Losing a marriage. Anything that life can throw at you. Come on you little beauties.

Stay on top. So it continued. There was only one team in it at that stage. The hosts' second goal came like a bolt out of the blue. Totally against the run of play. An innocuous looking free kick was arrowed into his own net by Facundo Sava. Fulham though, to their eternal credit, continued to carry the game to the opposition. Right up to the point where the Fat Lady exercised her tonsils. The tie was not yet over. A fortnight's breathing space existed for reflection and tactical readjustment. An opening skirmish does not a battle make.

Berliner Zeitung · Nummer 277 · Mittwoch, 27. November 2002 – Seite 32··

Berliner Zeitung

Sport

Abgehoben: Stefan Beinlich (2. v. r.) köpft den 1:0-Führungstreffer für Hertha BSC

Nicht gut, nicht schlecht

Hertha BSC rätselt, was vom 2:1-Sieg im Uefa-Pokal gegen den FC Fulham zu halten ist

VON MICHAEL JAHN

BERLIN, 26. November. Wenn ein Torjäger ins falsche Tor

UEFA Cup, third round, first leg.
Venue: Olympia Stadion. *Attendance:* 14,477.

HERTHA BSC, BERLIN (1) 2   FULHAM (0) 1
Hertha: Kuraly, Friedrich, Van Burik, Alves (Preetz 58), Goor, Marcelinho, Nene, Dardai, Schmidt (Simunic 58), Hartmann, Beinlich (captain) (Pinto 88). Unused subs: Fiedler, Sverrisson, Tretschok, Madling.
Fulham: Van der Sar, Finnan, Brevett, Melville (captain), Marlet, Sava, Malbranque (Inamoto 78), Djetou, Goldbaek (Boa Morte 45), Davis, Goma. Unused subs: Taylor, Clark, Knight, Wome, Stolcers.
Scorers: Beinlich 28, Marlet 53, Sava 68 (og).
Bookings: Preetz, Dardai.
Referee: Dick van Egmond (Holland).

There had to be an upside following the disappointment of the result. Later that evening, as a group of us embarked on an exercise of tonsil rinsing, some interesting FA Cup first round replay results began to permeate the airwaves. Of particular note was Queens Park Rangers being beaten by Vauxhall Motors 4–3 on penalties, after a 1–1 draw. At Loftus Road, no less. Shame.

In closing, mention must be made of the dubious sartorial tastes of the average Berlin football fan. Maybe it was the influence of the newly liberated eastern lands but the majority appeared to be locked onto a timewarp of a quarter of a century ago. An incarnation of seventies man. Mullet hairstyles abounded, as did flares, scarves tied around the wrist and denim jackets festooned with patches. Echoes of the hairy boot boy era. Compared to them the Hammersmith End on tour was at a fashion level approaching designer.

9: HIGH NOON

Fulham Ladies v 1 FFC Frankfurt – Sunday, 30th November 2003

A clash of the titans in direct competition with the Sunday roast. Winner takes all. In retrospect the meat and two veg came a poor second. The Women's UEFA Cup had arrived in the tranquillity of the Surrey heartlands. But it appeared to come at a price. There was a choice. Either witness the second meeting of two of the best in European ladies football. Or partake of a London derby at Highbury…

Forget the hyperbole surrounding the Premiership. A decision had already been made for me. Three decades before. And, right or wrong, all I had to do was continue along the road marked 'Fulham in Europe'. To a natural conclusion. No diversions, nor short cuts. Whatever the cost.

My family character trait of stubbornness is well defined. Despite that I could still see that our girls had a devil of a job on their hands. To come away with anything like a winning aggregate from the tie they had to overturn a two goal arrears from the first leg. Perfectly possible given normal circumstances. Yet, unfortunately, these were not.

A couple of factors appeared to conspire against our success. We were missing a brace of stalwarts resultant from situations arising from the first leg. No excuses, just consequences of incomprehensible refereeing decisions. The coach, Marieanne Spacey, was confined to the stand, having no contact with the players for the duration. Her misdemeanour was to have purportedly been spotted outside of the technical area. And our mercurial will-o'-the-wisp winger, Rachel Yankey, was serving a one match suspension. Seemingly for a yellow card given for a reckless tackle. God give me strength!

Pre-match advertising plus programme. Spot the blooper. 'Erster Frauen Fussball Club'?

Forgive me the pun about a level playing field. The pitch too was posing a problem. It was not conducive to the playing of flowing football. The effects of a thaw following the first frost of the winter, allied to the early kick-off, meant that the heavy roller was still being used on one goalmouth fifteen minutes before kick-off. The area behind the goal line could best be described as a quagmire. Not the best of situations, it must be said. All Fulham could do was put on a brave face and make light of it.

Which, to a great extent, is what they endeavoured to do. They got amongst Frankfurt from the off, continually taking the play to their opponents in an attempt to disturb their rhythm. The build up, although dictated by the need to score goals, still had to be structured. Measured, as the Germans' speed of movement and mobility on the break could not be allowed to dominate proceedings and, in doing so, cause inestimable harm to our chances. That approach allowed them to more than hold their own up until the interval Although no goals were on the scoresheet, Fulham would be attacking the drier end of the ground in the second period. That was sure to pay dividends. At least one hoped so.

Remain looking at the positives. But with association football being the type of game it is, within minutes it appeared to have gone pear shaped. Leaving the girls with a mountain to climb. Commitment to all-out attack in the final forty-five minutes allowed star striker Birgit Prinz to grab the opening goal. It not only gave Frankfurt the lead on the day but opened up a three goal advantage in the tie. Fulham were not to be denied and continued to pour forward in numbers. Their moment of glory came with ten minutes remaining. A blinding twenty-five yard drive from Dannii Bird beat Marleen Wissink, the visitors' custodian, all ends up. It was easily the goal of the game.

Hope sprang eternal to this Fulham breast. Miracles do sometimes happen. But anti-climax struck in the outstanding minutes. The accent on attack had produced tired minds and limbs. Which lead to instability at the back. Frankfurt profited from the situation, snaffling three goals—one from Pia Wunderlich plus a pair from Patrizia Barucha—very late on. Cruel.

Women's UEFA Cup, quarter final, second leg.
Venue: Kingfield. *Attendance:* 656.

FULHAM LADIES (0) 1   1 FFC FRANKFURT (0) 4
Fulham: L. Hall, K. Jerray-Silver, C. Yorston (C. White 81), J. Wright, M. Phillip (captain), K. Chapman, R. McArthur, R. Unitt, T. Waine (S. Duncan 60), M. Hickmott, G. Ritchie (D. Bird 60). Unused sub: S. Chamberlain.
Frankfurt: M Wissink, S. Minnert, L. Hansen, N. Kunzer (captain) (M. Wilmes 72), P. Wunderlich, T. Wunderlich, B. Prinz, R. Lingor, K. Kliehm (J. Affeld 67),

K. Zerbe, S. Albertz (P. Barucha 45). Unused subs: M. Krummenauer, S. Rastetter, B. Legrand, S. Weichelt.

Scorers: Prinz 50, Bird 80, P. Wunderlich 84, Barucha 86, 89.

Bookings: Yorston, Jerray-Silver.

Referee: Ms J. Palmqvist (Sweden). *Assistants:* Ms S. Borg, Ms H. Caro (Sweden).

Another dream sadly extinguished, the irony of which was not lost on me. A second European odyssey finishing on home soil, this time at Woking. The 7-2 overall aggregate scoreline was not a fair reflection of play over the two matches, I felt. What it did prove however, was that Frankfurt took their chances when they presented themselves, as befitting a quality outfit. For Fulham Ladies it had been a tremendous learning experience which, one hopes, they will be able to repeat. Sooner rather than later.

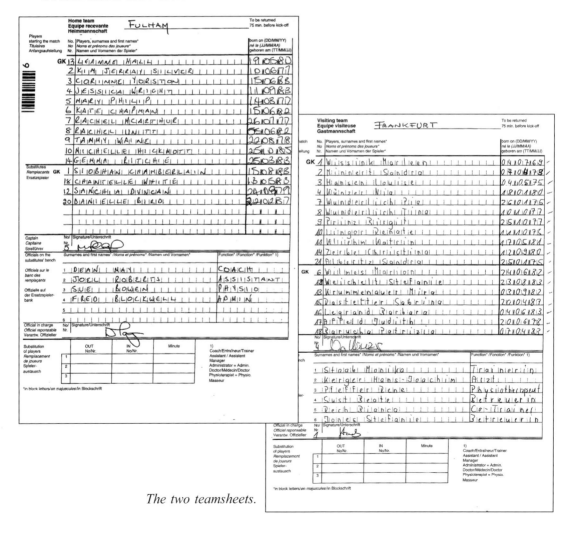

The two teamsheets.

10: PROUD

Bologna v Fulham – Tuesday, 13th August 2002

Sufficient for an entry into the diary of life. A statement that should be flagged, highlighted and underlined… Deep into the mists of time, the events of Martedi 13 Agosto 2002 are to be remembered and cherished by Fulham folk. Certainly long after this quintessential quill is done with chronicling, its owner pushing up the daisies. Put plainly but simply, it was the European coming of age for Fulham Football Club. As such the ensuing result is to be both documented and analysed. Before being placed in the annals of Lilliewhite history. And storage in the archives at our dearly beloved Craven Cottage. For time immemorial.

In the wider perspective this was so much more than just a game of football. The whole day was just that little bit out of the ordinary. Special. From early morning Bologna, citta della cultura, was invaded by two or three hundred free spirits. Fulhamish to the core. Emissaries in black and white. Presenting the modern face of our club to a larger audience in the best possible light. Just the idea of Fulham playing in a European Cup Final brought moisture to the eyes. You'd cross the globe to see that. Indeed one stout fellow had, jetting in from New Zealand to cheer on his favourites.

Prominently located at the centre of the plains of Emilia Romagna, Bologna is famous for a number of geographical features. It is primarily known for being the 'Clapham Junction' of the Italian rail network but it is also recognised for its architectural heritage and ancient artefacts. Which is a good way of describing what a number of our company resembled after the morning's exercise. An ascent of the taller of the two towers of 'Due Torri' involved panting and wheezing over one thousand steps. Having said that, the panoramic view at the top was absolutely breathtaking. The descent of same could be regarded as a healthy pre-lunch loosener. Guaranteed to induce a lengthy siesta afterwards. All part of the 'Fat City' experience.

Much later that evening, when we gathered in an outdoor café in the Piazza Maggiore to celebrate our good fortune, the toast was a lengthy one. It lasted until three o'clock the following morning and was complete with musical overtones. Simultaneously to imbibing, we were able to witness the preparations for a 'son et lumière' style pageant that was to be performed the following evening. One of the backing compositions was none other than *Blue Moon*. A serenade wasn't in it. So many West London voices harmonising in a beery yet joyous rendition. Intoxicating stuff.

Earlier we had been enthralled witnesses at a pulsating and captivating game of football. Latin temperament versus flair and spontaneity, the latter all coming from Fulham. Our resolution in the first half was total. The class shown in outmanoeuvring the Rossoblu in their own back yard reduced the home crowd to astonished silence at times. That Fulham had the audacity to take on and outwit a Serie A outfit at their own game, yet with elegance, style and panache speaks volumes for the character of the team. Conclusive proof if such were needed.

A roller coaster second forty-five minutes even managed to upstage that which had preceded it. Aided and abetted, one suspects, by a set of Hispanic officials, Latins all, who had a better understanding of, and forbearance with, the volatile and unremitting nature of calcio. The hosts twice wrestled the lead through 'sympatico' penalties. The first was given for a quite magnificent swan dive, the second involving a tug. A testing of shirt fabric. The plunge to the turf, if it had been performed by a leading exponent of the art such as Brian Phelps, should

CORPO DI POLIZIA MUNICIPALE

MARTEDI' 13 AGOSTO 2002

PARTITA DI CALCIO

BOLOGNA
FULHAM

029285

Rif. 00007

UEFA – INTERTOTO CUP 2002
BOLOGNA – FULHAM
Stadio Renato Dall'Ara. 13/08/02 20:30
Curva San Luca ospiti

Prezzo Euro 10,00
Prev. Euro 0,00

Match ticket. Note the number. Bonding with Fulham, or what?

Warning poster retrieved from the trees adjacent to the ground. "You can't park 'ere."

DIVIETO DI SOSTA
RIMOZIONE FORZATA

Bologna F.C. 1909
w w w . b o l o g n a f c . i t

INTERTOTO CUP 2002/2003
13/08/02 - STADIO "RENATO DALL'ARA" DI BOLOGNA – ORE: 20.30
FINALE-ANDATA

CALCI D'ANGOLO BOLOGNA				
1	2	3	4	5
6	7	8	9	10
11	12	13	14	15

CALCI D'ANGOLO FULHAM				
1	2	3	4	5
6	7	8	9	10
11	12	13	14	15

	BOLOGNA FC 1909		FULHAM
1	Pagliuca	1	Van Der Sar
2	Zaccardo	2	Ouaddou
4	Olive	3	Brevett
5	Castellini	4	Melville
7	Nervo	5	Goma
8	Colucci	6	Legwinski
9	Cruz	7	Marlet
10	Signori	8	Malbranque
15	Smit	9	Hayles
19	Falcone	10	Davis
23	Goretti	11	Boa Morte

	All. Guidolin		All. Tigana
	A disposizione:		
12	Coppola	13	Taylor
6	Gamberini	12	Collins
11	Bellucci	14	Inamoto
14	Ardito	15	Saha
20	Locatelli	16	Knight
21	Brioschi	17	Leacock
31	Meghni	18	Sava

Arbitro:
Iturralde Gonzales Eduardo (SPA)
Assistenti:
Lopez Villate-Guerrero Alonso
Quarto uomo:
Turienzo Alvarez

AMMONIZIONI	
Giocatore	Minuto

ESPULSIONI	
Giocatore	Minuto

MARCATORI	
Giocatore	Minuto

SOSTITUZIONI		
ENTRA	ESCE	MIN

Note:

Aove: official teamsheet. Below: the following day's headlines. Complimentary, one suspects.

INTERTOTO, FINALE D'ANDATA: GLI EMILIANI SI ALLONTANANO DALLA COPPA UEFA

Il Fulham beffa il Bologna al 90'

Non bastano le due reti di Signori dal dischetto: Inamoto e Legwinski siglano la rimonta londinese

CORRIERE dello SPORT — STADIO — CALCIO — MERCOLEDÌ 14 AGOSTO 2002 — 2

BOLOGNA-FULHAM 2-2 Il capitano illude i rossoblù. La squadra di Baresi pareggia a un minuto dalla fine

Bologna, Signori non basta

Doppietta di Beppe-gol (su rigore), gli inglesi rimontano due volte. Uefa più lontana

LE PAGELLE
Nervo trascina
Smit non delude

have scored a near perfect 9.9. All that was missing were a couple of pikes and a tuck. Such is the Italian way. It was up to Fulham to overcome such questionable practices to ensure further progress.

And overcome they did, consistently playing their way out of difficult situations. Junichi Inamoto, who had in my view almost achieved legendary status in just 104 minutes in a Fulham shirt, grabbed the first equaliser. Description of the strike reduces me to a feeling of total inadequacy. Two minutes after entering the fray as a substitute he went off on one of his runs from midfield. Literally bouncing off Italian tackles, he climaxed the move by despatching a precision ball low into the far corner beyond the despairing clutches of a surprisingly portly Pagliuca.

Ironically, the last futile challenge was delivered by Beppe Signori, potentially our penalty spot nemesis. Then, three minutes from time, the on song 'Monica' Legwinski latched on to a knock back and arrowed a daisy cutter into the opposite goalnet extremity. The visitors section of the Curva di San Luca just erupted. Absolute pandemonium. We were beside ourselves with glee. And exultation. Oh come and behold them, born the kings of football…

UEFA Intertoto Cup, final, first leg.
Venue: Stadio Renato Dall'Ara. *Attendance:* 23,620.

BOLOGNA (0) 2   FULHAM (0) 2
Bologna: Pagliuca, Zaccardo, Olive, Castellini, Nervo (Brioschi 82), Colucci, Cruz, Signori (captain) (Bellucci 85), Smit, Falcone, Goretti (Locatelli 70). Unused subs: Gamberini, Coppola, Ardito, Meghni.
Fulham: Van der Sar, Ouaddou, Brevett, Melville (captain), Goma, Legwinski, Marlet, Malbranque (Inamoto 62), Hayles (Saha 62), Davis, Boa Morte. Unused subs: Collins, Taylor, Knight, Sava, Leacock.
Scorers: Signori 54, 76 (both pens), Inamoto 64, Legwinski 87.
Bookings: Goretti, Nervo, Colucci, Legwinski, Saha, Davis, Boa Morte.
Referee: E. Gonzales (Spain). *Assistants:* L. Villate, G. Alonso (Spain).

It didn't end there. The last act of a memorable footballing evening came when our small convoy of coaches was returning to the main square. Much gracious applause from the home fans. Genuine appreciation of an outstanding performance. Grazie tifosi Bolognese.

One final observation. Bologna appeared to be closed for the month of August. Holidays presumably. There were 'chiuso per ferie' notices everywhere. Surely the inhabitants hadn't retreated because the Lilliewhites were in town? Just a thought.

11: OUT OF THE DARKNESS

Fulham v FC Haka – Saturday, 6th July 2002

And into the light. Both in a metaphorical and a footballing sense. Dazzled. Blinking. Increased illumination which also included an additional bonus. The first leg of a UEFA competitive fixture was to be contested at Craven Cottage. As one who had yearned for the day, how good it felt. A respectable sized crowd were of the same opinion, wending their respective ways along the tree lined avenues surrounding God's green acres. Coming to view what was potentially the last game at the ground before an enforced sojourn in urban Westwayland.

Put that notion on hold, at least for a couple of hours. We were gathered to immerse ourselves in the occasion. To pay homage to what generations of the Lilliewhite faithful had understood as home. Then the reality of the situation kicked in. If we were to leave let us at least go with a bang. The previous season's final home Premiership fixture against Leicester City had finished goalless. An anti-climax. A damp squib. A bit of a let down. Please don't let that situation occur again.

Low-key press coverage of one of the eventual Cup winners.

FULHAM

Your Official Fulham FC Matchday Programme **50p**

FULHAM versus FC HAKA
Saturday 6th July 2002 Kick Off 3.00pm

UEFA INTERTOTO CUP

adidas
Kit Sponsor

WESTERN UNION | MONEY TRANSFER
Community Match Sponsor

Match programme, which sold out on the day. Historical considerations plus the intrinsic value make it a must for collectors.

The Finns of FC Haka, in opposition that afternoon, were there to be taken, I felt. Although quite seasoned European campaigners, they had only just scraped past the Serbs from FK Obilic in the first round. All Fulham required was a little bit of patience and a touch of luck. The goals would surely come, I reasoned. Yet in retrospect it is funny how such a level of expectation can cloud one's judgement so. Blinded by the light I suppose. Manfred Mann's Earth Band if I remember correctly.

But a goalless stalemate? What had been conveniently overlooked in the original assessment were the effects of playing the first match of the season. Any season. A gentle work-out to help attain the required fitness. Perfectly reasonable for a pre-season friendly. But this was not. Yet Fulham stuck to the task with diligence. Their delightful possession play and crisp interpassing simply over-whelmed Haka. There were times when the Finns were reduced to bit part levels, playing follow-my-leader for most of the ninety minutes. Fulham's ratio of shots on goal was remarkable, chances either missing the vital final touch, being blocked by bodies, whistling narrowly wide or being denied by the heroics of Haka's Polish custodian Mihail Slawuta. Frustrating is stating the obvious.

UEFA Intertoto Cup, second round, first leg.
Venue: Craven Cottage. *Attendance:* 7,908.

FULHAM (0) 0   FC HAKA (0) 0
Fulham: Taylor, Ouaddou, Harley, Melville (captain), Goma, Davis, Marlet (Boa Morte 71), Saha, Sava (Hayles 61), Collins, Malbranque (Goldbaek 79). Unused subs: Hahnemann, Knight, Hudson, Legwinski.
Haka: Slawuta, Karjalainen, Pasoja, Ylonen (captain), Innanen (Vaisanen 79), Ristila (Aalto 63), Ruhanen (Koivuranta 70), Rantala, Kovacs, Okkonen, Kangaskorpi. Unused subs: Vilmunen, Koskinen, Torkkeli, Pasanen.
Bookings: Malbranque, Karjalainen, Ylonen, Okkonen.
Referee: L. Gadosi (Slovakia). *Assistants:* J. Suniar, M. Vindis (Slovakia).

Maybe it was not meant to be. Just one of those days. The perception had changed. We were off to Valkeakoski on a mission. Out of the darkness… Because of QPR's continuing pre-season commitments, should the club be successful in the land of the lakes, the home leg of the next round would also be played at Craven Cottage. A welcome stay of execution. Be thankful for small mercies.

12: HRVATSKA CONTINUUM

NK Dinamo Zagreb v Fulham – Thursday, 31st October 2002

Hajduk style infinitives had become a thing of the past. An historical component of English prose. Nevertheless, an ongoing flirtation with topics Croatian could be explained away as just another instance of the vagaries of life… Several hours spent in transit doing nothing but watch the pouring rain at Zagreb's Pleso airport en route from Split on Sunday 22 September gave no indication of an imminent return. Plenty of scope for idle thought but little else. The inclement weather conditions meant that plans for an exploration of the Medvednica slopes were put on hold until a more opportune moment. Likewise visiting the Hard Rock Café on Gajeva Ulica. Nor for a minute could one foresee a retracing of steps a matter of six weeks later. UEFA's mandarins having a giggle was the logical supposition.

A little bit of local knowledge does you good… Preparatory investigations revealed that the hard core of the Dinamo Zagreb support revelled under a less than savoury moniker. Contrary to those who have been schooled in the refinements of black and white. The BBB, or Bad Blue Boys were meant to be even more fanatical than the Torcida in Split. Yet, paradoxically, they were just the type that I could relate to, standing as they did for the virtues of tradition and honour. Action, rather than words. I just hoped that the assessment was correct as a clump round the head is not to be recommended at my age. Especially as experience warned to be ready to get the retaliation in first.

C'est la vie. Unlike their Dalmatian coast rivals, Dinamo's European jousts with English clubs had been few and far between. Their one major success was to have defeated Leeds United in the 1967 Fairs Cup Final. Before that there had

POSEBNI PRILOG

sn *sportske novosti*

Dinamo

Silvio Marić
& Robert
Prosinečki

10

najvećih

EURO

utakmica

The Dinamo magazine. Supplied with the 'Sportske Novosti' daily newspaper.

been a couple of occasions in the late fifties where they had entertained Birmingham in the original Inter Cities Fairs tournament. However, it may well have been that both were 'select' teams. In much the same way, Johnny Haynes and Jimmy Langley represented London in the same competition. But, beyond those instances, not a lot to concern oneself with.

The manufactured 'Croatia' Zagreb in the Champions League didn't even enter the equation. Thus Fulham's visit to the Maksimir Stadium was the first by a club from these shores for thirty-five years. Although Dinamo had just relinquished the leadership of their league before our visit, gut reaction intimated that, given the rub of the green, the Lilliewhites could be triumphant. To be able to continue riding the crest of a European wave would be to the benefit of all concerned. Or at least that was the theory.

One mustn't forget our venturesome intrepids in all this. We had reached the stage of the competition where club organised charters and two day stopover trips were making an impression on the numbers travelling independently. However, word did filter through of two separate expeditions emanating from SW6. The first group were flying to Trieste and continuing by car via Ljubljana in Slovenia. The second duo, elegantly lead by an irrepressible hostess, were using pastures new as a means of entry to the European mainland. A budget flight Stansted to Klagenfurt, thence by train to Zagreb Glavni Kolodvor. Having journeyed via Graz to Bratislava myself for the England games a couple of weeks earlier, one could understand the benefit of the Austrian route. Tremendously picturesque but one needed to wrap up well. It tended to be a mite chilly, especially in the evenings.

Many ultimately empty words of hostility were electronically transmitted in our direction beforehand. It was put down to no more than the usual unsettling psychology surrounding a European trip. In the event the Zagreb experience turned out to be no more unfriendly than a vicar's tea party. Not that one attends too many of those, you understand. The locals were just so downright sociable. Especially in the Hard Rock Café. In the two days that yours truly spent wearing the colours on the streets of the Croatian capital, there was not even a wayward glance in my direction. In fact the hour's march on matchday, from Jelascica Square in the city centre to the ground could be described as an interesting walk. Underwhelming even.

Spot the looney?

First sight of the Stadion Maksimir was of a grim, forbidding sort of place. A concrete fortress. A throwback to the days of communism. Intimidating perhaps, yet actual entry revealed that the security staff had recently attended a course at charm school. Suspicion was that they were preparing for the stereotypical English football fan abroad. Instead they got your scribe, denizen extraordinaire from the Hammersmith End, SW6. From a spot right behind the goal the flag was unfurled and there one stayed for the duration. To be entertained beyond my wildest dreams.

Enthralled. Enraptured. The fixture unfolding truly was a revelation. Many column inches detailing the delights of the occasion have been expended by the experts in the press. Using words and descriptive phraseology that your son of the terraces cannot hope to match. Personal summary states that the direction of the game's fortunes hinged around the expulsion of centre half Kristijan Polovanec for a professional foul around the half hour mark. From that point on Fulham simply took charge and had a field day. They utilised the advantage of having an extra man to deadly effect and, in doing so, achieved their best result and performance in Europe thus far.

UEFA Cup, second round, first leg.
Venue: Stadion Maksimir. *Attendance:* 25,000.

NK DINAMO ZAGREB (0) 0   FULHAM (1) 3
Dinamo: Butina, Sedloski, Smoje, Polovanec, Maric (captain), Agic, Mikic, Krznar, Balaban (Petrovic 64), Mitu, Olic. Unused subs: Turina, Bosnjak, Cesar, Mujcin, Kranjcar, Zahora.
Fulham: Van der Sar, Finnan, Brevett, Melville (captain), Marlet (Hayles 66), Boa Morte (Stolcers 72), Legwinski, Goma, Djetou (Inamoto 59), Malbranque, Ouaddou. Unused subs: Taylor, Knight, Clark, Wome.
Scorers: Boa Morte 37, Marlet 60, Hayles 79.
Bookings: Mitu, Finnan. *Sent off:* Polovanec 32.
Referee: E.I. Gonzales (Spain). *Assistants:* M. Nieto, E. Rozas (Spain).

Suffice it to say that there is one more significant comment that can be made about that glorious evening. Fulham's undefeated European run 1973-2002 now stands at fifteen games. Long may it continue. There is no other club in England that can touch such a statistic. Fact.

Still elated at the result, I returned to the land of mobile phones and the chattering classes safely the next day. Confident in the knowledge that any half decent scoreline at our temporary domicile would ensure that the life of Riley could be continued until well into the approach of the festive season. It's costing an arm and a leg but who cares. Financial accountability appears still to be a long way off. Six months on the European brick road already. Some going that. The record of winning two European trophies in one season is there to be broken. Although that last remark could be viewed as hyperbole, at this stage of the game I wouldn't bet against it.

Boa Morte
finds touch
as Fulham
enjoy stroll

Fulham in heaven
after Tigana's
tactical triumph

Boa Morte sparks
Fulham goal feast

Boa Morte ends his famine as
Fulham feast on Croatian spoils

Boa Morte
starts romp
for Fulham

Headliners. Unfortunately, Friday 1st November was a National Day in Croatia, so there was no local newspaper production. It would have been intriguing to have seen the match reports in Serbo Croat.

13: INSIDE TRACK

V.V. Ter Leede v Fulham Ladies – Saturday, 23rd August 2003

Neck and neck in the finishing straight. With everything to play for. An exciting scenario. Yet before a description of Fulham Ladies' crunch group fixture with V.V. Ter Leede, there is an admission to be made. The chapter has been constructed in an about face manner. Back to front. Call it what you will. The next paragraph could have been viewed as more relevant if included with the match report of the opening game. A local description of the immediate environs around Sassenheim has been saved until now. With good reason. A connection appears that is obviously Fulhamish.

The daily journey from the squad's Noordwijk seaside base through to Sassenheim involved moving through a panorama that could only be described as chocolate box. Low Countries charisma covering every metre. Windmills, canals, sit up and beg bicycles rattling over cobbled streets. You get the picture. Midway through the five kilometre 'easy ride' was a picturesque village called Voorhout. A smart sort of place. Plenty of money about judging from the motor cruisers moored beside the macadamised way. It also contained a football ground. Nothing special in that you may think. Yet this is where Edwin Van der Sar embarked upon his footballing career. His father was still employed in a business down the street from Roodemolen, so I was informed.

Some extra coaching for goalkeepers Siobhan Chamberlain and Holly Cox would have been appreciated but… There was the matter of Everton at Goodison Park in the Premiership on the same day. A fixture which yours truly would take a rain check on in the continuing quest for 'Fulham in Europe'. The decision had been made and was set in stone. It was to be Rijnland rather than Merseyside. What the heck.

Cut to the chase. Saturday 23 August at six in the evening local time became crunch time for further European aspirations. The stakes were high for the respective champions of Holland and England. A quarter final place awaited the group winners. Finishing second meant try again next time. Don't call us, we'll call you. The first half was hard, yet evenly balanced with a one-all scoreline at the interval being a reasonable reflection of play. Time to step up a gear. As the second period progressed the contest became increasingly more tense. Yellow cards were being brandished as if they were going out of fashion.

Fulham triumphed in the end because they kept their heads when others around appeared to be losing it. There was a price to be paid too. Both teams

Vanuit (richting) Den Haag
Vanuit Den Haag de N44 volgen. Deze gaat na Wassenaar over in de A44. Afslag Voorhout/Oosthout. Bij rotonde rechtdoor. Bij stoplichten rechtdoor. Na plm. 200 meter ligt aan de linkerzijde de ingang van het sportpark.
Vanuit (richting) Amsterdam
Via A44 (Amsterdam - Den Haag). Afslag Warmond, einde afrit linksaf. Bij stoplichten rechtsaf. Na plm. 200 meter aan de linkerzijde bevindt zich de ingang van het sportpark. Roodemolenweg 10, Tel: 0252 - 210174

Translation from the Dutch conveniently leads one straight to the clubhouse. Cheers.

finished with a player short. Jess Wright was stretchered off with a nasty looking ankle injury a minute from the end. It left the transgressor going in to test the bath water upon receipt of a second yellow card. The first tentative steps into Europe had been taken. The group stage examination had been passed. Marieanne Spacey's class of 2003 had emerged with flying colours.

UEFA CUP

Landskampioenen vrouwenvoetbal

Dinsdag 19 augustus Aanvang 19.00 uur
TER LEEDE - FC Cordu Anenii Noi

Donderdag 21 augustus Aanvang 19.00 uur
TER LEEDE - Ki Klaksvik

Zaterdag 23 augustus Aanvang 18.00 uur
TER LEEDE - Fulham Ladies FC

vv Ter Leede
Sportpark Roodemolen
Roodemolenweg 10
Sassenheim

Toegang gratis

Tournament poster. Word blindness is also apparent here, too.

UEFA Women's Cup, third round, group 8.
Venue: Sportpark de 'Roodemolen'. *Attendance:* 500 approx.

V.V. TER LEEDE (1) 1   FULHAM LADIES (1) 3

Ter Leede: B. Van Dalum, J. Van der Laan, C. Burger, D. Koster, E. Scheenard, M. Noom (captain), S. Dijkhuizen (J. Poldervaart 79), S. Muller, L. Van Leuwen, I. Witteman (P. Hogewoning 77), S. Van Eyk (S. Drommel 24). Unused subs: J. Wolfram, M. Huizer, K. Legemate, C. Stolk.

Fulham: S. Chamberlain, K. Jerray-Silver, C. Yorston, J. Wright, M. Phillip (captain), K. Chapman, R. McArthur (S. Duncan 41), R. Unitt, T. Waine (S. Flint 86), R. Yankey, G. Ritchie (M. Hickmott 62). Unused subs: H. Cox, C. White, R. Bennett, D. Bird.

Scorers: Yorston 8, 85, Van der Laan 45 (pen), Yankey 60.

Bookings: Van der Laan, Scheenard, Noom, Muller, Jerray-Silver, Yankey. *Sent off:* Noom 90.

Referee: K. Elovirta (Finland).

FINAL TABLE

	P	W	D	L	F	A	Pts
1. Fulham Ladies	3	3	0	0	20	2	9
2. Ter Leede	3	2	0	1	14	3	6
3. F C Codru	3	1	0	2	6	20	3
4. Klaksvik	3	0	0	3	3	18	0

Scorers: Waine 5, Yorston 3, Chapman 3, Yankey 3, Jerray-Silver 2, Duncan 1, McArthur 1, Hickmott 1, Flint 1

Being Fulhamish, there just had to be a downside somewhere. The Toffees' 3-1 winning scoreline at Goodison could not be ignored. It should have put a damper in the victory celebrations. Instead it was left on the back burner while your scribe engaged in a passable imitation of boogieing the night away. Agreed, it was more akin to Come Dancing. Except the dress code was minus organza, sequins or tulle. For me, what had been a most illuminating six days drew to a most satisfactory conclusion. Frankfurt would be next. The expectancy levels were rising…

The time abroad had been quite enlightening in a linguistic sense. Another Dutch word had been assimilated. 'Roodemolen' means 'Red Mill'. So there you go.

14: HOPE SPRINGS ETERNAL

Fulham v A.S. Roma – Wednesday, 21st March 1973

Fulhamish to a tee. Especially as our opponents that long ago midweek evening at Craven Cottage hailed from the Eternal City. A.S. Roma were eagerly awaited illustrious visitors to our Thamesside patch. Then, as now, they were one of the leading lights from Serie A. Buoyed by our opening result in the tournament, a goalless draw in Como, the prediction was that Fulham could certainly give Roma a game. Yet, given the Italian predisposition for close marking, whether it would be an entertaining spectacle to watch was another matter entirely.

Unfortunately my fears were realised. Given the slightly jaundiced view of a Hammersmith End regular, from what can be remembered of the contest, it was nothing to write home about. No glowing report then. The Italians compressed the play from the outset. They blocked, obstructed and bodychecked. The fabric of the Fulham kit was minutely examined by Roman fingernails. Export of the tactics that were regularly employed back in their homeland. From the terraces, it was not just frustrating, but boring to witness. Somnolence personified.

Then, having roughed Fulham up a little, they had the audacity to take the lead. Renato Capellini knocking home after eighteen minutes certainly was not part of the script. Yet it acted as a wake-up call. Our Lilliewhites were rightly indignant. Upper lip bristling, they tackled their duties with renewed vigour. An equaliser wasn't long in the making. Only six minutes had elapsed before Les Strong caressed the back netting with a perfectly angled header from a Cutbush cross.

Classic. With parity achieved both teams beavered away industriously until the interval, though no more goals were forthcoming. Time to draw breath. Regrettably the second half subsided into the morass of midfield mediocrity. Any attempt by Fulham to instigate flowing football or to knock the ball about was immediately smothered by the all-enveloping use of catenaccio. From an English perspective it was an insult to our intelligence. In truth it came as a blessed relief when the final whistle put an end to proceedings.

In opposition.

Anglo-Italian Tournament, group 2.
Venue: Craven Cottage. *Attendance:* 7,712.

FULHAM (1) 1   A.S. ROMA (1) 1

Fulham: Mellor, Cutbush, Callaghan, Mullery (captain), Went, Richardson, Strong, Earle, Mitchell, Lloyd, Barrett. Unused subs: Pinkney, Horne, Fraser, John Conway, Webster.

Roma: Ginulfi, Bertini, Peccennini, Rocca, Bet, Santarini (captain), Cappellini, Salvori, Muiesan (Orazi 70), Morini, Franzot. Unused subs: Liguori, Sulfaro, Scaratti, Di Bartolomei.

Scorers: Cappellini 18, Strong 24.

Booking: Santarini.

Suffice it to say that Roma's approach to the fixture was not at all impressive. Which would be stating the obvious. It might be argued that, on the night, Fulham didn't appear to possess the guile to break the Italians down. Overall the game was bitterly disappointing. So much more had been expected from Roma. No doubt lessons had been learned from the display so all that could be done was to move on. Face the upcoming trip across to Turin with a positive attitude. For the faithful, hope always did spring eternal…

FULHAM FOOTBALL CLUB LTD

CRAVEN COTTAGE, STEVENAGE ROAD, S.W.6.
TELEPHONE: 01-736 5621/7035. TELEGRAMS: FULHAMISH, LONDON, S.W.6.

TEAM SHEET

FULHAM		A.S. ROMA
Peter Mellor	1	Ginulfi Alberto
John Cutbush	2	Peccenni Franco +
Fred Callaghan	3	Liguori Liborio
Alan Mullery	4	Rocca
Paul Went	5	Bet Aldo +
John Richardson	6	Santarini Sergio + (Capt)
Les Strong	7	Salvori Elvio
Steve Earle	8	Morini Giorgio
John Mitchell	9	Cappellini Renato +
Barry Lloyd	10	Muiesan Lucio
Les Barrett	11	Franzot Walter
		Substitutes
Alan Pinkney	12	Orazi Angelo +
Stan Horne	13	Sulfaro Michel Angelo
John Fraser	14	Scaratti Francesco
John Conway	15	Bertini Giovanni
Malcolm Webster	16	Di Bartolomei

+ Italian Internationals

Fulhamish to a team-sheet.

15: FOUR IN THE MORNING

Aigaleo v Fulham – Saturday, 27th July 2002

W as not only a successful musical composition in the seventies era. It would also adequately describe the nocturnal arrival and departure movements through Athens airport for the three old soldiers on their latest perambulation towards the outposts of UEFA competition. Aiming ever higher.

Apart from the traffic and pollution, for most tourists a visit to the capital of the Hellenes is usually quite a culturally enriching experience. On the other hand, for the average football fan travelling from these shores, Athens is generally a hostile environment. One speaks from hard experience, having been badly slapped about there prior to an England fixture some years back. A friendly match at that. Broadly speaking, your scribe and the Athenians are like oil and water. We do not mix. This was Fulham however… Positive vibes are beginning to permeate a hard bitten exterior.

Paradoxically enough, this is where ironies continue. After a wait approaching thirty years for a Fulham away game in European competition, the arrival brings a sense of déjà vu. The initial couple of venues, Tehtaankenttä and Apostolos Nikolaidis had both previously been visited with England Under-21s. Such is life. The trip to Panathinaikos in June 2001 is one that I would rather forget. Our intermediates suffered a humiliating 3–1 reversal with both John Terry and Luke Young in receipt of their marching orders. A memory to be discarded.

Naturally, one hoped for better things against Aigaleo. They, like ourselves, would be on foreign ground, having migrated from the intimacy of Korydalos to the heights of Ambelokipi. Our protection of the single goal lead gained in what was the imagined swansong before a temporary demise from Craven Cottage was of the utmost importance to our immediate aspirations. First things first though.

We were booked on a holiday charter out of Gatwick on the Friday night. Four hours in the cramped company of the bucket and spade brigade was not the most relaxing way to spend the wee small hours of a Saturday morning. Yet, if needs must. Also the air fare was of bucket shop dimensions. Reasonably cheap. That has to be a major personal consideration. The supply of funding may have to stretch through to a projected UEFA Cup Final but also include England trips. A financial treadmill. All on a pension of course. Ain't life just grand at times. Yet it has got to be done.

Any initial misgivings posed by a footballing visit to Athens in support of an English team had long since dissipated by departure day. An upbeat mood prevailed

Έδρα: Δημαρχείου 66 - 68, ΑΙΓΑΛΕΩ ΑΤΤΙΚΗΣ
Γραφεία: Ιερά Οδός 286 - 288
Εμπορικό Κέντρο «ΣΥΝΤΡΙΒΑΝΙ»
122 43 ΑΙΓΑΛΕΩ ΑΤΤΙΚΗΣ
Τηλ.-Fax: 53.16.883
E-mail: paaea@acci.gr
Α.Φ.Μ.: 094493582 - ΦΑΚ.: 510111 - ΔΟΥ: ΦΑΕΕ ΑΘΗΝΩΝ
ΑΡ.Μ.Α.Ε.: 36578/05/Β/96/41 (1996)

Π.Α.Ε. «ΑΙΓΑΛΕΩ Α.Ο.»

EGALEO F.C.
v
FULHAM F.C.

UEFA INTERTOTO CUP – THIRD ROUND SECOND LEG
SATURDAY 27TH JULY 2002 9:00PM

NENAD BIKIĆ	45	1	EDWIN VAN DER SAR
KONSTANTINOS PAPOUTSIS	2	2	ABDESLAM OUADDOU
GEORGIOS ALEXOPOULOS	6	3	JON HARLEY
DIMITRIOS MEIDANIS	5	4	ANDY MELVILLE (C)
NIKOLAOS NIKOLOPOULOS	17	5	ALAIN GOMA
DANIEL EDUSEI	3	6	SYLVAIN LEGWINSKI
IOANNIS CHRISTOU	14	7	STEVE MARLET
IOANNIS SKOPELITIS (C)	20	8	STEED MALBRANQUE
ENDINGUE JEAN DENIS WANGA	8	9	LOUIS SAHA
GEORGIOS FOTAKIS	16	10	SEAN DAVIS
IOANNIS CHLOROS	7	11	LUIS BOA MORTE
MAHAMADOU SIDIBE	33	12	JOHN COLLINS
EMMANOUEL PSOMAS	22	13	MARTIN HERRERA - GK
DEJAN STEFANOV	10	14	FACUNDO SAVA
ANASTASIOS AGRITIS	9	15	BARRY HAYLE
ABRAAM SIMEONIDIS	13	16	ZAT KNIGHT
MICHAEL CHATSIS	19	17	BJARNE GOLDBAEK
JEAN PIERRE ANTONETTI	21	18	ANDY STOLCERS

Referee	Bossen Ruud (Hol)
Assistant Referee	Veluwen van Jan Willem (Hol)
Assistant Referee	Wassink Rob (Hol)
4th Official	Geneos Christos (Gre)
UEFA Delegate	Paulo Bergamo (Italy)

ΠΟΔΟΣΦΑΙΡΙΚΗ ΑΘΛΗΤΙΚΗ ΑΝΩΝΥΜΗ ΕΤΑΙΡΕΙΑ

...BOUT FOOTBALL

...OTO

ΑΙΓΑΛΕΩ
FULHAM F.C.

3ος ΓΥΡΟΣ

27 ΣΑΒΒΑΤΟ 2002
ΙΟΥΛΙΟΥ
ΓΗΠΕΔΟ ΠΑΝΑΘΗΝΑΙΚΟΥ "ΑΠΟΣΤΟΛΟΣ ΝΙΚΟΛΑΪΔΗΣ"

Σ 286-288 - Α.Φ.Μ. 094493582 - Δ.Ο.Υ. ΦΑΕΕ ΑΘΗΝΩΝ

GATE 6 ΘΥΡΑ

throughout the whole excursion despite the level of match policing on the day. Totally over the top in my opinion. For some there were benefits to even that situation. The stormtroopers of law and order were introduced to some good old-fashioned terrace ditties. Very quaint. Distinctly Fulhamish.

Nine of our blithe spirits were on the overnight service to El. Venizelos, the newly constructed principal Athens airport. Whilst the majority headed for the Glyfada beaches on arrival, we trio of reprobates were based centrally, in a hotel near Omonia Square. The Saturday morning hours were spent indulging in yet another of my passions. An idiosyncratic tour of Hard Rock Cafés around the world. The establishment was located in one of the seedier parts of the port of Piraeus, at the junction of Etolikou and Papastratou. It was definitely of 'moody' status, yet it had to be checked out.

It never ceases to amaze from where elements of the club's hardcore support arrive to be a part of what is deemed to be an important fixture. One well known face endured a five hour ferry passage up from the caldera of Santorini. He was displaying the after effect of a few days in the Aegean sun. Red legs was not in it. Another august gentleman, complete with equally intrepid grandson had interrupted their vacation in Bodrum. A marine hop to Kos then a domestic flight onwards. The merest of day trips, the Turkish authorities had been informed. The spirit of adventure is not dead. It is thriving amongst the wayfarers of West London. On the night the overall turnout of nearly eighty fans was much appreciated by the team. What might be the numbers present in Montbeliard, that much nearer to home, one wonders.

Wish you were here beside route Leoforos Alexandras, a transport artery out to the north-east. Saturday evening, 27 July 2002. Not the best of outlooks it must be admitted. Traffic congestion outside, claustrophobic police restrictions in. Yet we wouldn't change it for the world. Fulham easily held the upper hand throughout the ninety minutes, exhibiting real touches of class when it mattered.

It's all Greek to me. The bottom line is that Fulham are through.

Faced with both the hosts' rumbustious approach, not dissimilar to that shown at the Cottage, and an energetic and volatile home following, the Lilliewhites controlled events in a disciplined manner. If only they could have done something about the Aigaleo club song issuing from the loudspeakers. Describing the melody as banal would be an understatement.

The opening strike was the Greeks' only credible effort during the whole of the first half. When Ioannis Chloros lashed in a cross shot after twenty-four minutes our spirits dipped a fraction. But only momentarily. We travelling faithful are nothing but optimistic. Ten minutes had elapsed before a return to parity on the night. The rightful restoration of our aggregate lead came as a result of a slide rule cross by the effervescent Luis Boa Morte. A deft yet masterful glancing touch by 'Bob' Marlet and it was exodus for the home side.

Time then for a nostalgic sing-song amongst the Thamesbank contingent. Lead by some of the more mature among our number, "Jimmy Conway", "Filthy Blue" and "Stevie Earle" featured prominently, if a little tunelessly. Funny how a goal in Europe can be so uplifting. Even with worn out vocal chords like mine. Tactical second half substitutions featuring Bjarne Goldbaek, Barry Hayles and Andrejs Stolcers all played a part in achieving what was a very satisfying result for all concerned.

UEFA Intertoto Cup, third round, second leg.
Venue: Apostolos Nikolaidis Stadium. *Attendance:* 1,200 approx.

AIGALEO (1) 1   FULHAM (1) 1
Aigaleo: Bikic, Papoutsis, Alexopoulos, Meidanis, Nicolopoulos (Agritis 45), Edusei, Christou, Skopelitis (captain), Wanga (Chatsis 60), Fotakis (Stefanov 70), Chloros. Unused subs: Cidibe, Simeonidis, Psomas, Antonetti.
Fulham: Van der Sar, Ouaddou, Harley, Melville (captain), Goma, Legwinski (Goldbaek 71), Marlet (Hayles 71), Malbranque (Stolcers 84), Saha, Davis, Boa Morte. Unused subs: Collins, Herrera, Sava, Knight.
Scorers: Chloros 24, Marlet 34.
Referee: R. Bossen (Holland). *Assistants:* J.W. Van Veluwen, R. Wassink (Holland).

For the record, that's now eight games unbeaten against European opposition. Como, Roma, Torino, Bologna, Haka and Aigaleo. Seven draws, one win. Some statistic that. The ensuing late night victory party plus Sunday lunch in a taverna on the island of Aegina left yours truly with a nasty attack of Grecian collywobbles. Gut rot in fact. An uncomfortable journey home as a consequence but who cared. Straight on down to Rail Europe to book return tickets to Montbeliard via Paris and Belfort. A lot costlier than at first anticipated. Allez Les Blancs!

16: SPITTING FEATHERS

Fulham v HNK Hajduk Split – Thursday, 3rd October 2002

Is one of the occupational hazards encountered whilst counting chickens. Therefore, if anyone was under the impression that the difficult part of winning this two-legged tie had been achieved in the balmier climes of Split a fortnight before, think again. Tres vite. There was still a very uncomfortable opening forty-five minutes at Loftus Road to be sat through. Or squirmed if that is a more fitting description of the movement of one's derriere on the seat. Admittedly that is only from a fan's perspective but I can empathise with what it must have been like in the dugout.

I appear guilty of getting ahead of myself also. Being victorious in the Intertoto Cup had still not prepared the majority of Lilliewhite faithful for the unaccustomed novelty of European competition at the higher level. Progress had to be earned. It was not sufficient just to turn up. In direct contrast, the appearance of several

dozen Croats in the South Africa Road, downing four packs like there was no tomorrow, was a throwback to English football's bad old days, Yet it didn't prevent them from giving whole hearted and noisy support for their team. Which is deserving of admiration when you consider the sanitised state of the average Premiership customer in general nowadays. Or is that comment seen as an old feller trying to put the world to rights?

The Dalmatian fans' raucous devotion to their cause reached new heights after only five minutes when they became ecstatic. Vlatko Djolonga not only provided them with the lead but equality in the tie. Fulham gritted their teeth, dug deep and began to build again. Redemption within fourteen minutes. A 'Bob' Marlet equaliser gave parity on the night. That state of affairs did not last long. Hrvoje Vejic eased the Croatians in front again with half time beckoning. As in the first leg, Steed Malbranque became Fulham's saviour, converting a somewhat controversial penalty two minutes before the break.

In an ideal world that situation would be seen as typically Fulhamish. Yet our favourites could not rest on their laurels during the second period. Both teams strove to be the ultimate victors and a distinct edge of frustration crept into the play. The Croatians' tendency to prostrate themselves at every available opportunity

began to irritate Fulham. As did the Italian referee's proclivity to wave yellow cards at all and sundry. But we survived to fight again…

UEFA Cup, first round, second leg.
Venue: Loftus Road. *Attendance:* 9,162.

FULHAM (2) 2   HNK HAJDUK SPLIT (2) 2

Fulham: Van der Sar, Brevett, Melville (captain), Marlet, Sava (Hayles 74), Boa Morte (Inamoto 67), Malbranque, Knight, Legwinski, Davis, Ouaddou. Unused subs: Taylor, Clark, Collins, Wome, Leacock.
Hajduk: Pletikosa (captain), Djolonga, Vejic, Bule, Carevic (Mise 84), Deranja (Racunica 71), Andric, Vukovic, Srna, Miladin, Neretljak. Unused subs: Runje, Piric, Balic, Brgles, Gudelj.
Scorers: Djolonga 5, Marlet 19, Vejic 39, Malbranque 43 (pen).
Bookings: Brevett, Melville, Carevic, Srna, Neretljak.
Referee: S. Farina (Italy). *Assistants:* M. Ivaldi, L. Maggiani (Italy).

…In pastures nearly new. The reward for the victory was another visit to Croatia. No complaints, we'll just have to do it all over again in Zagreb. My one query of the night was of a statistical nature. The official attendance of 9,162 was more than doubled by that given in the press the following morning, A dubious looking 18,500 is almost a full house at Loftus Road. No way was the gathering anything approaching that number.

UEFA CUP / Disputed spot-kick spares Tigana's men in a nerve-tingling tie
Steadfast Steed
Malbranque keeps cool to swing it for Fulham

17: LIFE WITH THE LIONS

FC Sochaux-Montbeliard v Fulham – Wednesday, 7th August 2002

The return of the Francophile. International duty apart, it seemed an awfully long time since the foray over to Le Touquet in the summertime of 2001. The digestive tracts were going through gastronomic cold turkey. They were crying out for the delights of escargots au beurre, moules marinière or a dish of cassoulet. All particular favourites of mine. Anything as a damage limitation to the intestinal ravages of Athens belly. So come on. Indigestion tablets at the ready. Let's go.

Ain't no stopping us now. We're on the move. Whichever sceptics imagined that the Intertoto was a two bob competition should try being a regular member of our clutch of European adventurers. For us, cynicism is not on the agenda. Round by round organising of the next sortie across the water has become progressively more difficult. Compressed timeframes between fixtures didn't exactly assist matters either.

But what the heck. We're Fulham. Never say die. Where there's a will. Determination is our middle name. Travel itinerary options for the semi-final, second leg down to the Franche Comte region, near the Swiss border, appeared to be many and varied at first glance. Yet because of the existence of so much bureaucratic complexity, in the event it became an exercise of picking straws. And personal preference. Air, rail or automobile. Paris Est; Dijon; Heathrow; Besancon; Basle; Belfort; Paris Lyon; Stansted. You want Montbeliard? Unscramble that little lot. Although there was choice for the independent traveller costs were appreciably higher when compared to the greater distances involved in reaching Greece or Finland.

The realisation of spiralling transport charges was somewhat softened by the knowledge that we were following easily the most exciting team to come out of West London this century. By a country mile. We were also able to venture to the domain of Peugeot carrying the luxury of an inner confidence, brought about by a trio of factors.

Initially, that precise left foot strike from Sean Davis, the opener at our Loftus Road lodgings, had caused the first reverse that our opponents had suffered in their UEFA travels this season. The first two results on the road were viewed as Sochaux being reasonably strong defensively. Two-one at Zalgiris Vilnius followed by three-nil at Synot was a further indication of attacking capability. The wheels, therefore, appeared to have come off the Joyriders' vehicle as they attempted to negotiate W12 7PA, giving Fulham the upper hand.

Secondly, was one alone in thinking that Les Bleus' stumbling performance during the World Cup would filter down to their club sides. And, in doing so, affect their domestic performances. The magnificence of quality bordering on arrogance, that had been evident in French football since 1998, would take a time to resurface after such a crushing disappointment. If it ever did.

The final and most important reason was us, the fans. The faithful that were following the Lilliewhites along the European trail would sway the tie in our favour, one felt. At the present time, just to be an Englishman abroad fills one with an immense pride. Departure on the Tuesday morning 05.15 Eurostar was with a beaming smile. Fit and able to have a tilt at the Parisian attitude on the way through. En avant mes amis. Groove on down the line. Bypass Chattanooga. Montbeliard here I come.

Doesn't time fly when you're having fun. Another three intermediate destinations had been added to an ever growing list of itineraries. Lyon; Geneva; Nice. For Fulham read inventive, cavalier or sophisticated. And that's only the supporters! Notwithstanding that, the forecast for matchday Mercredi was decidedly inclement. However, if you'll pardon the pun, a little bit of weather wasn't going to dampen Lilliewhite spirits by a single iota. Not one jot. Water testing was scripted so we just got on with it. The bouquet of a good Tigana is a beautiful thing. Formidable.

Beforehand, on the Tuesday evening, yours truly had clandestinely mingled with the locals. Watching the hosts conducting a full blown training session. Comprehension of a fair amount of spoken French has its advantages. The general atmosphere was subdued and reticent. Various shortcomings were identified within the Lions ranks, particularly the guardien, the goalkeeper. Now, if somebody like your scribe could spot such, so too could our Three Musketeers. And be in a position to do something about it.

The opening half followed an almost predictable pattern The psychological ploy of the spider and the fly. Draw in then hit on the break. Fascinating yet ultimately sterile, Fulham calmly and confidently containing infrequent goal attempts from FCSM. The second period, on the other hand, unfolded all too differently. A triple home substitution on 54 minutes was the turning point. Sochaux began to lose the plot and shoot themselves in the foot at the same instant. One of the newcomers, a young starlet, came on to the pitch with only one thing on his mind. That of putting himself about. Big time. Suffice it to say the ploy backfired. He lasted twenty-five minutes, accumulating two yellow cards and a red. Bad mistake. Au revoir.

Fulham, as we knew they could, produced a classic forty-five minutes. The opening goal, a looping header from Sylvain Legwinski, was a textbook strike. 'Monica' really did give it some cranium. Our second was also something to drool over. Barry Hayles went on a never ending run, beating player after player. He

Club magazine. On sale in town.

tous les projets lancés ou encore à l'étude. L'audit analysera chaque projet pour en déterminer la faisabilité, le calendrier mais surtout le coût, rigueur budgétaire oblige. Seul le TGV-Est est officiellement confirmé.

5

Sochaux : au revoir l'Europe !

4

finished by planting the ball into the Gallic onion sack with unerring accuracy. Eruptions of delirious happiness from the ninety-three travelling diehards. Victory on aggregate by three clear goals. C'est magnifique.

UEFA Intertoto Cup, semi-final, second leg.
Venue: Stade Bonal. *Attendance:* 11,000.

FC SOCHAUX-MONTBELIARD (0) 0   FULHAM (0) 2
Sochaux: Daguet, Tall, Saveljic, Flachez (captain), Monsoreau, Oruma (Pedretti 54), Chedli, Mathieu, Isabey, Boudarene (Pagis 54), Zairi (Silva 54). Unused subs: Martinovic, Daf, Raschke, de Carvalho.
Fulham: Van der Sar, Ouaddou, Brevett, Melville (captain), Goma, Legwinski, Marlet, Malbranque (Inamoto 59), Saha (Hayles 67), Davis, Boa Morte (Collins 73). Unused subs: Herrera, Knight, Sava, Lewis.
Scorers: Legwinski 63, Hayles 72.
Bookings: Pedretti, Chedli, Boudarene, Brevett. *Sent off:* Pedretti 79.
Referee: M. Wack (Germany). *Assistants:* Messrs Salver and Schiffner (Germany).

Allow oneself the pleasure of drifting off and dozing. Perchance self-indulgently to dream. Fulham in a European Cup Final. It takes a bit of getting one's head round. And when, god willing, we make the UEFA Cup, the likes of Anderlecht, Lazio, Porto and Werder Bremen really will be in exalted company. Settle down, old son. You'll be giving yourself one of those palpitations next.

Afternote: Am I right in thinking that the original Three Musketeers were Athos, Porthos and... Aftershave. Just a thought.

18: DI LAGO

A.C. Como v Fulham – Wednesday, 21st February 1973

Dependant on one's own perspective, the Como fixture could be considered as Fulham's first in Europe proper. The Anglo-Italian Tournament was a recognised UEFA competition at the time. English teams did not enter the Intertoto Cup in those days either. What is not up for debate is the fact that the venue was probably the most picturesque stadium that Fulham had ever played in. Situated on the lake shore with an alpine backdrop as a setting the panoramic vista was positively breathtaking. It took another twenty years or so before the aptly named Paradise FC, Dover Sports Ground, St. Lawrence Gap, Barbados assumed the mantle in the mind's eye of your scribe.

In purely financial terms the Torneo Anglo-Italiano, brainchild of the late Gigi Peronace, was not a resounding success. The concept, that of bringing together two different footballing cultures, was spot on but generally attendances were poor. Its decades of existence, involving primarily professional clubs but also leading semi-pro outfits spasmodically from 1970 to the early nineties, never really took off. On-field indiscipline marred some of the encounters and the experiment of using English referees in Italy and vice versa somehow just didn't click. There was a high spot however. It was provided by the travelling English who regularly ventured across to the Apennines in droves. Speaking personally there are fond memories of the tournament, especially a sortie across in May 1971 which doubled up as a honeymoon. Sampdoria versus Huddersfield Town, along with Internazionale against Crystal Palace, are forever viewed in a rosy hue. Happy days.

That which had gone before was of little consequence to the dozen or so pathfinding diehards who boarded the boat train at Victoria on the morning of Tuesday, 20th February 1973. A trip of some considerable adventure lay ahead. Our £25 return ticket was to open the door to a voyage of exploration in the grand manner. Europe, and the Italian Lakes in particular, were about to become acquainted with the Fulhamish experience.

As the train picked up speed crossing the Thames, the first of many tinctures began to loosen the tonsils. Twenty hours later, our eventual arrival at Como San Giovanni would be robustly toasted with the last remnants of the supplies of beverage. But that was still in the future… Nowadays, a couple of hours on an aircraft with a cheap flight to either Milan or Turin plus no more than an hour on Ferrovie Stato (FS) would be all that was needed to reach the environs of Lake Como. That type of transport option wasn't available during the seventies.

Train-boat-train transit via Folkestone Harbour, Calais Maritime, Hazebrouck, Lille, Valenciennes, Mauberge, Charleville-Mezieres, Longwy, Thionville, Metz, Strasbourg, Colmar, Mulhouse, Basle, Bellinzona and Chiasso occupied many long and weary hours. A leisurely trundle, with the accent on trundle, stopping at what seemed like every misbegotten halt across Northern France, journeying almost to the Luxembourg border before turning south then east through Switzerland to reach the destination. Immensely satisfying, one imagines, to a railway buff. Yet we were not. But at the end of the long and metalled road, was the prospect of watching our beloved Lilliewhites in Europe.

Time passed slowly. Consumption of prodigious amounts of alcohol caused much jollity and jackhammer after-effects. Occasional decoration of a passing quai when the gastric juices were uplifted by forces of gravity. Nearly losing one of the party on the gare at Thionville. A true intrepid, he got off to stretch his legs. The carriages were shunted to a different platform, and without his glasses, he had difficulty in finding them again. A right spectacle. Snow-covered mountains by moonlight. A picture postcard scene. Finally… Number twos by numbers in

Match poster.

what passed for the stazione facilities. Pooh! Almost a chapter in itself. We had arrived.

As a tourist town Como was straight out of the top drawer. Spectacular. Just the type of place to bring the other half for a romantic few days. Except for the train journey, that is. Early sighting of the mist on the lake gave the whole scene a surreal quality. Hold on though. We were there for a football match. Travelling fans, especially the detested English camp followers, are not supposed to appreciate anything resembling a panoramic vista, let alone remember sufficient features to be able to adequately describe it upwards of thirty years later.

Looking back, another memory is that the locals just could not get their head around our being there. Notwithstanding that it was the host club's first appearance in European competition, the very notion of how anybody could travel for nearly a day on a train to see Como play was alien to them. Our polite response of only venturing to watch Fulham just confused the issue further. At least the ideals of the tournament were being met through the footballing small talk.

Approaching three o'clock. A whole hearted rendition of the National Anthem was being sung. Players and fans alike. An embodiment of togetherness… After such a build up it could only go one way. Downhill. The ninety minutes play was somewhat anticlimactic. A goalless draw. Perverse. All that way for coconuts. By way of an explanation, it was the first time that Fulham had encountered calcio. More frustratingly they were not able to prise open a mean home defence. In spite of almost total domination the one all important goal just would not come. Even more annoying was the after-match press conference admission by the hosts that they were only interested in not losing. A sad state of affairs, yet indicative of the Italian psyche of the time.

A very rare ticket stub if the prevailing circumstances are considered. Only a handful of the faithful were present and, in a more personal sense, it was the start point of a journey of discovery that has so far lasted three decades.

Anglo-Italian Tournament, group 2.
Venue: Stadio Sinigaglia. *Attendance:* 3,111.

A.C. COMO (0) 0   FULHAM (0) 0

Como: Cipollini, Cattaneo II, Danova, Chinellato, Magni (captain), Cerantola (Gamba 78), Cattaneo I, Pozzato, Bellinazzi, Amadori, Turini. Unused subs: Mascella, Galetti, Correnti, Frigerio.
Fulham: Mellor, Cutbush, Callaghan, Mullery (captain), Went, Dunne, Jimmy Conway, Earle, Mitchell, Pinkney, Barrett. Unused subs: Fraser, Strong, Moreline, Richardson, Webster, Lloyd.
Bookings: Chinellato, Cerantola.
Referee: K. Burns (Dudley).

Note: Receipts at the turnstiles that afternoon amounted to 3,743,700 lire. However, modern day conversion of that sum into Euros wouldn't even pay some Premiership players' wages for a week. Such is the march of progress.

Eight weeks later we were to return to the same Lombardy-Piemonte region. To the Stadio Comunale in Turin for a 1–1 draw against Torino. Also memorable in its own way but, after the marathon trek to and from Como, just another European fixture.

Stadio Sinigaglia—an aerial view, as depicted in the Fulham programme for 17th February 1973, against Sheffield Wednesday.

19: BETWEEN A ROCK

Fulham v Hertha BSC, Berlin – Thursday, 12th December 2002

And a hard place. A very hard place in this instance. Positively granitic on both counts. All of sixteen days had elapsed since the single goal defeat in the Olympia Stadion yet my enthusiasm for the outcome of the second leg had not diminished. To my mind the two-one scoreline equated with almost a blank canvas. That was crying out to be added to with a flourish. Several flourishes in fact. The feeling was that Fulham still had enough in the tank to overcome disciplined opponents. Yet pride cometh…

Leaving one with grazed knees and a dented ego. In terms of our opposition's technical capabilities, 'disciplined' could have been substituted by any manner of phrases. Like 'superbly organised'. Or 'Teutonically efficient'. Even 'utilisation with a modicum of fuss'. Yet descriptions like these were to be expected. They came with the territory. The third round of the UEFA Cup was not for mugs. Nor was it for the faint-hearted. It was, though, a yardstick. A measure of how far Fulham Football Club had travelled in the six intervening months. Progress had been marked. The European profile was blossoming. Yet doubts lingered. Would Hertha provide our Alamo? Were our favourites about to stumble when the orange groves of Seville appeared not to be that far away?

Regretfully the answer to both questions was in the affirmative. On the night Hertha were just too tactically astute. Lucky yes, but in this game you make your own luck. Chances were made and spurned by both teams yet, as a spectacle, the temperature never really rose above lukewarm. There was one performance that stood out like a beacon on a frosty evening, that of referee Pierluigi Collina. With his gleaming pate and staring eyes he cut an impressive figure. Delivering a masterclass, respected by players and gallery alike. No complaints. The best way to depart the European stage was with dignity. Which, in a nutshell, is exactly what transpired. Fulhamish.

UEFA Cup, third round, second leg.
Venue: Loftus Road. *Attendance:* 15,161.

FULHAM (0) 0   HERTHA BSC, BERLIN (0) 0
Fulham: Taylor, Finnan, Brevett (Goldbaek 70), Melville (captain), Marlet, Boa Morte, Malbranque, Djetou (Legwinski 45), Davis (Inamoto 61), Goma, Wome. Unused subs: Clark, Knight, Herrera, Willock.

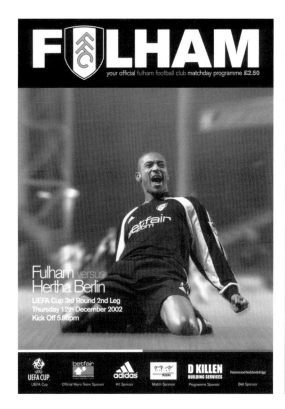

Hertha: Kiraly, Friedrich, Goor, Luizao, (Preetz 80), Marcelinho, Simunic (Van Burik 7), Nene, Dardai, Neuendorf (Zecke) (Schmidt 72), Hartmann, Rehmer (captain). Unused subs: Sverrisson, Fiedler, Tretschok, Marx.
Bookings: Melville, Inamoto, Friedrich, Nene, Neuendorf (Zecke).
Referee: P. Collina (Italy). *Assistants:* C. Puglisi, S. Saglietti (Italy).

Looking back along the European trail, in the final analysis only about a dozen of the faithful had managed all fourteen matches. Financial retribution too, would strike at some stage in the future. Enough of that because the time between July and mid December 2002 will always be looked back on as a time to savour. Heartfelt thanks go to our Lilliewhites for allowing this old reprobate, for one, to realise a dream. One that lasted, in all its glory, for precisely one hundred and sixty days. Ich bin ein Fulhammer. Auf wiedersehen.

Being the way I am, conscientious and a stickler for detail, there is still a statistical oddball that requires an answer before this chapter is finished. Just who was the visitors' number twenty that night? The official teamsheet and teletext had him listed as 'Andreas Neuendorf'. On the other hand the match programme indicated 'Zecke', as did the name on the back of his shirt. For literary peace of mind therefore, he shall be referred to as 'Neuendorf (Zecke)'. Unless anyone can throw further light on the subject, that is.

20: DIE WOCHENENDE

1 FFC Frankfurt v Fulham Ladies – Sunday, 2nd November 2003

Something for. Or words to that effect. The opening days of November delivered your scribe on another little continental sortie. Ostensibly to witness the Fulham Ladies tackling the next stage of their European adventure. Resultantly, a rain check had to be taken from the Liverpool Premiership fixture at our Shepherds Bush lodgings. In times past, the Sabbath used to be reserved for activities ecumenical or of relaxation. At leisure. Not the case any more due primarily to the all encompassing demands of television. A square eyed dominatrix. Yet personally, having become a champion of ladies football, it would have been sacrilege not to have presented myself in Frankfurt-am-Main on the second day of the month.

Whether viewed from one's masculine or feminine side, in my case the lure of 'Fulham in Europe' has become too strong to resist. Whether it is seen as my being totally committed to the cause or in the initial stages of being classified as a fruitcake is open to conjecture. Supposition is that the jury is still out… Too much meaningless chatter. Let's have it. Away to the Bundesrepublik's commercial centre on the northern bank of the River Main. As distinct from Frankfurt-an-der-Oder which has the delights of Poland beckoning from the opposite shore. The town of Slubice to be more precise.

Enough of the geography lesson. Organising a weekend break in Germany centred around a Sunday afternoon women's fixture also offered a fair degree of scope for taking in a local game on the Saturday. So it transpired and, on the back of some research beforehand, I was able to watch the Hesse derby between Offenbach Kickers and 1 FC Eschborn. An electric atmosphere plus one of the coaches being banished to the stand for assaulting the dugout wall with his fist were overriding memories. And, as an Englishman abroad, the availability of a match programme. Such simple desires…

Sorted. On to the Sonntag for another dose of Fulham in Europe. The three months since the group stage in Sassenheim had literally flown by. Supporter presence was now required at a compact little stadium in the suburb of Rödelheim, set amid the leafier, more deciduous outskirts of Frankfurt. Outward transit from the Hauptbahnhof on the U-bahn was interesting. Relaxing too, for it allowed time and space for reflection and thought. Emergence from subterranean level revealed tram tracks down the middle of the highway. Old fashioned and quaint, yet refreshing. The seven minute stroll to the Stadion am Brentanobad from the tram halt at Fischstein was somewhat novel too. There was even better to come.

Match ticket. Other than the relevant seat information, the remaining graphics were used on both match poster and programme.

Using both the follow my nose routine and a well established sense of direction produced an all-embracing feeling of ambience. Akin to that felt when ambling through Bishops Park en route to Craven Cottage.

The calm before… Arriving at the venue the feeling changed. There was a different presence. Vastly different. No welcoming committee of volunteers and helpers as had been the case in Holland. This was definitely no ordinary ladies game. Even the restrained friendliness was at arm's length. The reality of the situation created an emotional tension that manufactured a knot in the stomach. And, in the case of yours truly, heartburn. Of the acute variety. Quite so. This was a Women's UEFA Cup quarter final, first leg after all. The stake were high. Extremely high.

The heartburn was nowt to do with the previous evening's Ruby Murray either. It was at this point that I realised just how involved in the outcome of the game I had become. One of the team's defensive stalwarts, Kim Jerray-Silver, was out, suspended for accruing two yellow cards in the games at Ter Leede. Our rearguard had been redeployed to accommodate the suspension. Rachel Unitt, who I believe possesses the sweetest and most constructive left foot in ladies' football, was moved from the midfield into defensive duties. A sensible tactical move.

From the opening whistle 1 Frauen Fussball Club put Fulham under exceedingly heavy pressure. They produced a brace of heartstopping goalmouth escapes within the first couple of minutes. So when the hosts opened the scoring after seven minutes, Karin Kliehm slotting home after a neat bout of interpassing, it came as no real surprise. Fulham, though, were made of sterner stuff. They immediately went on the offensive which soon paid dividends, Another three minutes elapsed before they drew level with a quite superb goal, Rachel McArthur gloriously smashing in a testing cross from Rachel Yankey. What delight! My roar

Inside the magazine cover image:

Ausgabe 25 / 26. Oktober 2003

Anpfiff
Die FFC-Frauenfußball-Zeitung

Bundesliga
1. FFC Frankfurt –
1. FC Saarbrücken

Termine
Statistik · Infos
Saison 2003/2004

WM-Story
Deutschland bejubelt
seine Weltmeisterinnen

FFC-Personality
Steffi Jones

FFC II
Dritter Tabellenplatz

FFC III
Toller Start in die
neue Saison

FFC IV
Verjüngtes Team im Pech

FFC-Mädchen
Starker Aufwärtstrend

Saison 2003/2004   www.ffc-frankfurt.de

Club magazine, just one item amongst a surprisingly large amount of merchandise on sale.

of appreciation and acclaim suddenly stilted as I fought to prevent my dentures from flying into orbit. The scales had been balanced.

Much application and hard work from Fulham typified the remainder of the half. One apiece at the interval reflected well on our girls. They shall not pass. Thus far it was a job well done. On the evidence of the first forty-five, our opponents had lived up to their billing as quality material. The speed of some of their passing and movement off the ball had been absolutely inspirational. During the second period they managed to improve on that. A magnificent diving header from Sandra Albertz on fifty-seven minutes plus a lucky prod to a loose ball from Birgit Prinz twelve minutes later providing them with a two goal cushion. Fulham to their credit refused to give in and played their hearts out.

Women's UEFA Cup, quarter final, first leg.
Venue: Stadion am Brentanobad. *Attendance:* 4,400.

1 FFC FRANKFURT (1) 3   FULHAM LADIES (1) 1

Frankfurt: M. Wissink, S. Minnert, L. Hansen, N. Kunzer (captain), P. Wunderlich (J. Affeld 65), T. Wunderlich, B. Prinz, R. Lingor, K. Kliehm (M. Wilmes 89), C. Zerbe, S. Albertz. Unused subs: S. Rastetter, B. Rech, B. Legrand, P. Barucha, S. Weichelt.
Fulham: L. Hall, C. Yorston, J. Wright, M. Phillip (captain), K. Chapman, R. McArthur, R. Unitt, M. Hickmott (G. Ritchie 72), R. Yankey, S. Duncan, C. White (T. Waine 72). Unused subs: S. Chamberlain, S. Flint, D. Bird.
Scorers: Kliehm 7, McArthur 10, Albertz 57, Prinz 69.
Bookings: Kliehm, Wright, McArthur, Yankey, Waine, Spacey.
Referee: S. Focic (Croatia). *Assistants:* N. Logarusic, L. Krajic (Croatia).

In summary, it was a match worthy of the occasion. Before closing, however, there is a little something that needs to be got off my chest. Too long in the tooth to be spouting vitriol or spitting the pips out of sour grapes, I am nevertheless concerned when fair play appears to be missing. The Croatian match officials, especially the one with the unfortunate sounding surname, were party to some really bizarre decisions in my view. In particular was the banishing of Marieanne Spacey to the stand which marred a fascinating tussle. For me to witness that apparent transgression twice within twenty-four hours was unusual, to say the least. The ratio of yellow cards brandished also seemed a tad unequal. One-to-five gives totally the wrong impression about the game, making a mockery of an honest afternoon's toil.

Say no more. A difficult, though not insurmountable task lies ahead in the second leg. Fulham have the benefit of an away goal and Frankfurt do creak at the back when put under sustained pressure. There's still all to play for. The Fat Lady hasn't even begun to oscillate her larynx. The weekend didn't finish there. A Monday afternoon return to Heathrow, followed by omnibus and rail connections deposited your wordsmith outside the Recreation Ground, Aldershot about an hour before kick-off. Our reserves were now centre stage. C'mon you whites!

21: SINGIN' IN THE RAIN

Fulham v NK Dinamo Zagreb – Thursday, 14th November 2002

Look on the bright side. With my son alongside me to watch his first Fulham match in what seemed like ages this really was a bit of a family affair. Moral support for the old man possibly, but who cared. His had been a more regular presence on the Hammersmith End during the dark days. Indeed he seemed moderately surprised that Don Mackay wasn't manager anymore. Conveniently forgetting the cup excursion to Old Trafford under Keegan of course. But he was there, one of a hardcore gathering of the faithful. Willing Fulham on to a place in the next round of the UEFA Cup.

Our glorious Lilliewhites' goal-scoring deluge in the Stadion Maksimir a couple of weeks before was miniscule compared to what the elements contrived to produce that evening. The heavens opened with a vengeance, It bucketed down. Even the comparative luxury provided by forty quid-a-head front row seats on the

South Africa Road stand was of little defence given the conditions. We were soon soaked to the skin. Most definitely wet bums on seats. Yet pleased to be there. No worries. The terrace ditty reveals that you sing when you're winning. Well, we did. Harmonise that is. Whilst witnessing a victory.

But not without a struggle. Croatians are nothing but proud. Almost, but not quite, on a par with our Englishness. Their teams do not roll over and readily accept defeat. Even when facing an uphill struggle to overturn a three goal deficit. All credit to Dinamo Zagreb. Without sounding condescending, they came and gave it a go. It wasn't enough in the end but they did provide stern opposition to our favourites. In fact, for over half an hour of the second half they held the upper hand with a one goal lead. Ivica Olic whacked a cracking drive past the outstretched grasp of Edwin Van der Sar six minutes after the break.

Fulham didn't overhaul that score until right at the death. Despite playing some purposeful and determined football, they were getting no reward until Steed Malbranque struck two minutes from the end. It was followed by a Luis Boa

Morte effort in the very last knockings, deep into time added on. Five goals to one on aggregate. It set me up for a fine fish supper on the way home. Mmm. Tasty on both counts.

UEFA Cup, second round, second leg.
Venue: Loftus Road. _Attendance:_ 7,700.

FULHAM (0) 2   NK DINAMO ZAGREB (0) 1
Fulham: Van der Sar, Finnan, Brevett, Melville (captain), Inamoto (Malbranque 63), Clark (Djetou 72), Sava (Marlet 59), Boa Morte, Legwinski, Goldbaek, Goma. Unused subs: Taylor, Ouaddou, Wome, Stolcers.
Dinamo: Turina, Smoje, Sedloski, Cesar, Agic, Olic, Krznar, Kranjcar (captain) (Juric 76), Mitu, Mikic, Balaban. Unused subs: Butina, Mujcin, Zahora, Petrovic, Bosnjak, Drpic.
Scorers: Olic 51, Malbranque 88, Boa Morte 90.
Bookings: Smoje, Cesar.
Referee: L. Duhamel (France). _Assistants:_ A. Dutheil, P. Bombart (France).

Satisfaction guaranteed. This being in Europe was becoming decidedly moreish. Twelve down and… We were ready for whatever the Third Round draw would bring. Singin' and winnin' in the rain. Doopey doo doo doo…

Boa Morte the last action hero as Fulham find finishing touch

22: ALL AROUND THE WREKIN

FC Haka v Fulham – Sunday, 14th July 2002

Tours par excellence. Courtesy of a trio of Thames Bank old-timers. This could run and run… Fulham in Europe, to use a canine euphemism, is just the Dog's Danglies. For which us forty to seventy somethings have waited an inordinately long time. Patiently. Twenty-nine years and three months since a trip to the Stadio Comunale, Turin for an Anglo-Italian fixture in April 1973.

European competition may not mean a great deal to the current administration or to the vast majority of our modern day support but, believe me, there are Hammersmith End veterans who used to go misty eyed just at the thought of it. And still do. So when, at the 2001–2002 season's Ewood Park finale, the realisation dawned that the club were finally in amongst it, short hairs on many wizened and weatherbeaten necks stood erect at the prospect.

Three days later, the delights of a Far East endurance test were beckoning for yours truly. Not much time to organise. No problem. The lads were instructed to sort out a trip in my absence. As economically as possible. Yet reasonably direct. With several grand to be spent in Korea and Japan one didn't need to shell out another large wedge upon returning. Or that was the thinking. Naturally the boys came up trumps. Saturday morning BA flight to Stockholm, overnight ferry to Turku, thence a leisurely Sunday meander through the lakes up to Valkeakoski. By train or hire car as the fancy took us. In style. Couldn't be better. A class package for sure.

Ironically though, your scribe must be the only Fulham fan who had already visited Tehtaankenttä. October 2000 saw a couple of hundred itinerant English supporters there watching our Under-21s. A 2–2 draw in front of a paltry 1,426 spectators. No Sean Davis. It was before his time in the proudest shirt of all, not making his debut until the following year. Curiously enough, it was in the return fixture versus Finland, at Oakwell. What one remembers about the event was a large mill chimney behind one goal which belched pollutants into the atmosphere for the duration of the game. Nearby Tampere has been described as the 'Manchester of Finland' If that is the case, then surely Valkeakoski must be the equivalent of Oldham.

Enough of the preamble… A longed for Saturday morning. Check documentation, dust down the special events scarves, unwashed in thirty years, and be off. The outward airborne leg was as literally hundreds that had preceded it, so our arrival at the Swedish capital's Arlanda airport was the real origin of our European

KÄSIOHJELMA 2002
FC Haka VS Fulham FC
SU 14.7.2002 KLO 19.00

WALTIKAN WAUHTI-ILLOISSA!

18.7. TOMI MARKKOLA
25.7. ANTTI KETONEN JA
       NELJÄN SUORA
1.8.   LEA LAVEN

RANTAHOTELLI
WALTIKKA
VALKEAKOSKELLA
TERVETULOA!

Veikkaus
liiga

Intertoton 2. kierroksen 2. osaottelu

FC Haka - Fulham FC

14.7.2002
Tehtaan kenttä, Valkeakoski

Huom! Vaarallisten esineiden ja alkoholin tuominen kielletty.
Portilla suoritetaan UEFA:n määräysten mukainen sisääntulotarkastus

K-katsomo rivi **5** paikka nro   0096   **15€**

Kun on peli, niin Tehtiksellä tapahtuu

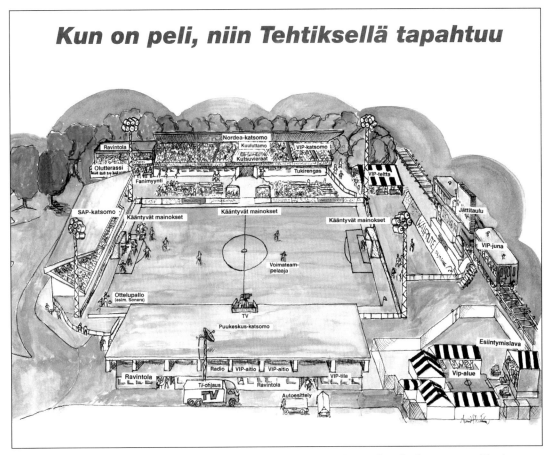

Tehtaankenttä–a schematic. Our travelling support was housed in the bottom two blocks behind the left hand goal. That stand had been constructed in the sixteen months since my first visit. Before, it had been just an open terrace.

extravaganza. A few ambling hours taking in the architecture around Stockholm harbour on a glorious summer's day was but the prelude to a dream. A warm evening and the ferry Amorella elegantly left port on a nine hour crossing to Turku via Mariehamn in the Aland Islands. The surface of the Gulf of Bothnia was like a millpond making it quite the smoothest nautical passage ever experienced. In conjunction with the effects of the midnight sun, the voyage could only be described as entrancing. Mesmeric even.

Easy like Sunday morning. After checking in an adjacent quayside hotel it was unanimously agreed to let Finnish Railways do the business on the penultimate leg, rather than utilising a hire car. There was a direct service from Turku Satamma to Toijala, the nearest railhead, some twenty kilometres from our destination. Toijala was where the planning suffered its one and only hiccup. What a place. In the middle of nowhere, or so it appeared. So quiet that even the tumbleweed was

JALKAPALLOILU

Mainio Haka piinasi Fulhamia

VELI-MATTI PARKKINEN / LEHTIKUVA

FC Haka–Fulham 1–1
Fulham jatkoon 1–1

La

▶ Tin
Marj
iloin

Måndag 15 juli 2002

SPORT

Sportredaktionen 09-12531, sport@hbl.fi

Haka utslaget trots bra insats

När den ene inte gör det, så

| Erotuomari: Tony Asunmaa ....7 | Erotuomari: Mika Koskinen ....8 | Erotuo |

ILTALEHTI **URHEILU**

Huttunen kuumana ottelun jälkeen

"Tuomari ei uskaltanut antaa punaista korttia"

Hakan taival Intertoto-cupissa päättyi perisuomalaisella tavalla. Tehottomuus maalin edessä kostautui. Viikko sitten päädyttiin maalittomaan tasatulokseen, eilen Valkeakoskella molemmat osuivat kerran.
Lontoolainen Fulham jatkaa cupissa 1–1-pelin jälkeen vieraemaaliaönpällä

vasta toinen pelimme tällä kaudella, Tigana arvioi.
Hakan joukkueesta onnistuivat eilen lähes kaikki. Ensijaksolla pirteimmät olivat nuori laitalinkki Innanen ja laitapuolustaja **Harri Ylönen**. Myös toppari **Juha Pasoja** pärjäsi yllättävän hyvin liuk-

Above: newspaper headlines in Finnish and Swedish. Right: the usual suspects—Hammersmith End reprobates on tour.

absent. The advertised local bus timings defied logic but we waited, slightly baffled, for one to arrive. And waited. Etcetera. Eventually our chosen mode of transport deigned to turn up. At a time specifically reserved for the Monday-Friday (Ma-Pe) timetable. A blessed relief. Twenty minutes later we rolled into Valkeakoski. Still some six and a half hours before kick off.

Further proof, if proof were needed, that even one's mid-term memory is becoming debilitated with age came upon sight of our hosts' bijou little premises. Adjacent was Tervasaari, a massive paper mill complex housing at least four chimneys. So much for a solitary provider to the ozone hole. Funnily enough, UPM, the mill's owners and one of Haka's shirt sponsors provide newsprint for one of our fruity daily tabloids. Fruity? Try the currant bun.

Over the next couple of hours the dribbling into town of some 120 of our most loyal was heartwarming to watch. As had the English in Japan, the Fulham faithful arrived from all points of the compass. Except for the official party, independents to a man. The level of support that should be appreciated. Pre-match supposition that if Fulham scored, overall it should be enough to win the tie proved correct. In truth, it has to be said that we had seen better performances from our favourites, Haka putting us under severe pressure towards the end. Never mind, aggregate victory on the away goal was still most satisfying. Well worth a wait of approaching half a lifetime.

UEFA Intertoto Cup, second round, second leg.
Venue: Tehtaankenttä. *Attendance:* 3,444 (sell out).

FC HAKA (0) 1   FULHAM (0) 1
Haka: Slawuta, Karjalainen, Koskinen (Aalto 54), Pasoja (Vaisanen 75), Ylonen (captain), Innanen, Ristila, Popovitch, Rantala, Okkonen, Kangaskorpi (Torkkeli 82). Unused subs: Vilhunen, Ruhanen, Pasanen, Koivuranta.
Fulham: Taylor, Ouaddou, Harley, Melville (captain), Goma, Legwinski (Boa Morte 56), Marlet, Davis, Saha, Collins (Knight 78), Malbranque (Goldbaek 89). Unused subs: Sava, Van der Sar, Hayles, Stolcers.
Scorers: Marlet 46, Ristila 66.
Bookings: Ylonen, Innanen, Goma, Boa Morte.
Referee: E. Laursen (Denmark). *Assistants:* B. Hansen, F Rasmussen (Denmark).

Happy Monday. A long 'un spent in glorious transit. Wearing permanent smiles all the way back to Heathrow. So far so good. Now let's do it all again for Athens. And Montbeliard or Stad Mesto. On into the UEFA Cup. Having at last joined the European merry-go-round on merit, let's make damned sure that we don't get knocked off before our time.

Visiting team / Equipe visiteuse / Gastmannschaft: FULHAM FC — To be returned 75 min. before kick-off

No.	Players (surnames and first names)	born on (DD/MM/YY)
GK 1	TAYLOR MARK	04/09/71
2	OUADDOU ABDES	01/11/78
3	HARLEY JON	26/09/79
4	MELVILLE ANDY	29/11/68
5	GOMA ALAIN	05/10/72
6	LEGWINSKI SYLVAIN	06/10/73
7	MARLET STEVE	10/01/74
8	DAVIS SEAN	20/09/79
9	SAHA LOUIS	08/08/78
10	COLLINS JOHN	31/01/68
11	MALBRANQUE STEED	06/01/80

Substitutes / Remplaçants / Ersatzspieler:

GK 13	VAN DER SAR EDWIN	29/10/70
12	SAVA FACUNDO	07/03/74
14	BOA MORTE LUIS	04/08/77
15	HAYLES BARRY	17/05/72
16	KNIGHT ZAT	02/05/80
17	GOLDBAEK BJARNE	06/10/68
18	STOLCERS ANDY	08/07/74

Captain No. 4

Officials on the substitutes' bench:

	Surnames and first names	Function
1	TIGANA JEAN	MANAGER
2	DAMIANO CHRISTIAN	AST. MANAGER
3	PROPOS ROGER	FITNESS
4	PEYTON GERRY	GK COACH
5	PALMER JASON	PHYSIO
6	BEVAN ALAN "PUDSEY"	KIT

Home team / Equipe recevante / Heimmannschaft: FC HAKA — To be returned 75 min. before kick-off

No.	Players (surnames and first names)	born on (DD/MM/YY)
GK 30	SLAWUTA MIHAIL	10/10/77
3	KARJALAINEN LASSE	22/10/74
4	KOSKINEN JUCCA	29/11/72
5	PASOJA JUHA	16/11/76
6	YLONEN HARRI	21/12/71
7	INNANEN MIKKO	08/09/82
10	RISTILA SAMI	15/05/74
14	POPOVITCH VALERI	18/05/71
15	RANTALA JUCCA	01/08/72
20	OKKONEN JARKKO	05/09/78
22	KANGASKORPI JUUSO	04/09/75

Substitutes / Remplaçants / Ersatzspieler:

GK 1	VILHUNEN MIKKO	23/08/80
8	AARTO IIRO	19/07/77
9	VAISANEN VILLE	19/07/77
11	RUHANEN JUKKA	16/01/71
16	TORCCELI TOMMI	19/07/71
20	PASANEN JARKKO	04/11/73
23	KOIVURANTA TARMO	05/04/66

Officials on the substitutes' bench:

	Surnames and first names	Function
1	HUTTUNEN OLAVI	HEAD COACH
2	HARTONEN KARI	ASS. COACH
3	PAASIO OLLI	TEAMLEADER
4	MYYRA KARI	KITMAN
5	TAKANIEMI JOUCO	PHYSIO
6	RASILAINEN PAAVO	DOCTOR

Teamsheets. 'Pudsey' hits the big time.

Confessions from a sad statto. For what seems like an absolute age, the following list of teams was repeated, parrot fashion. Over and over again so it wouldn't be forgotten. Ever. Reipas Lahti; Ararat Erevan; FC Den Haag; Eintracht Frankfurt; Anderlecht. West Ham's opponents from their unsuccessful run to the 1975–76 European Cup Winners Cup Final. Five names that were imprinted on my soul, keeping me constantly on my toes. For all of twenty-seven years.

Until our turn. Living the dream. FC Haka; Aigaleo; FC Sochaux-Montbeliard; Bologna; Hajduk Split; Dinamo Zagreb; Hertha BSC, Berlin. Such recollections. Memories and images that remain freeze framed in the mind. And will be so until departure on that final journey through the heavens.

23: STAIRWAY TO DREAMLAND

Fulham v Bologna – Tuesday, 27th August 2002

Saving the best until last is a maxim well worth adhering to. Yet the scenario that is documented here is something that us Cottage faithful of long standing could only have dreamed about in turbulent years gone past. Now it was upon us. You had just to pinch yourself to ensure that you were awake. And that what your imagination had identified as a fantasy was in fact reality.

The excellent draw that Fulham had crafted in the Stadio Renato Dall'Ara a fortnight before was but a few steps up the stair. The passage of fourteen days in which to overcome the strengths and weaknesses of the opposition was a prelude to further ascent. Towards a hallowed summit. At long last a European trophy was within the club's grasp.

Tantalisingly close. Aside from the opening two Premiership fixtures the preparation time had been well utilised. Loftus Road on a balmy August evening became the seemingly unlikely stage for European glory. The resolve of the Lilliewhites was apparent in the first few minutes. Only twelve had elapsed before Junichi Inamoto opened the scoring. Deadlock broken. Three-two in front on aggregate. The Thamesside boys were on the up. Black and white flew proud.

Bologna, as we with long memories knew of old, were nothing but combative opponents. Four yellow cards plus an equaliser from Tomas Locatelli were testimony to both Latin temperament and determined approach. The interval and a few sacred moments to draw breath and revise tactics from the safety of the inner sanctum.

So far, so good. Four minutes into the second half and the game as a contest appeared effectively to be all over bar the shouting. Another brace of goals for our rising son from Nippon and Bologna had been simply blown away. Never to come back. Reduced to also-ran status by the magnificence of it all. Fulham comfortably in cruise control. Inamoto's second goal, just seventy-five seconds into the half was an absolute peach. Worth the admission money alone.

Circumspection in triumph. It had come to pass. As the victorious Fulham players, along with an equally excited chairman, cavorted across the emerald carpet, it was time to take stock. UEFA Intertoto trophy winners at the first attempt. Another dream fulfilled. After the years of watching our favourites plying their trade around the nether reaches of the Football League this was indeed a moment worth savouring. Truly delightful. To be eulogised over by future generations of the Fulhamish faith.

FULHAM

your official fulham football club matchday programme £2.00

Fulham versus Bologna

Intertoto Cup Final Second Leg
Tuesday 27th August 2002
Kick Off 7.30pm

UEFA Intertoto Cup, final, second leg.
Venue: Loftus Road. *Attendance:* 13,756.

FULHAM (1) 3   BOLOGNA (1) 1
Fulham: Van der Sar, Finnan, Brevett (captain), Knight, Goma, Inamoto (Malbranque 72), Marlet (Saha 72), Legwinski, Sava, Davis (Collins 73), Boa Morte. Unused subs: Taylor, Melville, Hayles, Ouaddou.
Bologna: Pagliuca, Zaccardo, Olive, Castellini, Nervo, Colucci, Cruz, Signori (captain) (Bellucci 60), Falcone, Locatelli (Frara 87), Paramatti (Smit 76). Unused subs: Coppola, Gamberini, Goretti, Meghni.
Scorers: Inamoto 12, 46, 49, Locatelli 35.
Bookings: Finnan, Legwinski, Olive, Nervo, Colucci, Paramatti.
Referee: M. Busacca (Switzerland). *Assistants:* F. Buragina, G. Lucca (Switzerland).

Satisfaction. We had it. By the cupful. Our entry to the UEFA Cup had been realised. Friday 30th August would herald our immediate destiny.

INTO EUROPE / Tigana's Japanese gamble pays off as Londoners make

Three-star Inamoto seals it for Fulham

World Cup idol finishes Italian job

This big o us, in Sir B

By COL

Gripping stuff; but no Bologna tactic could keep Inamoto in check last night

Let us close this volume with a succinct yet nevertheless accurate statement. During season 2002–03, the only British football team to win a European trophy was…Fulham Football Club. Fact.

* * * * *

Boldly dressed in black and white.
He did follow Fulham.
The Thames flows on...